4/14

THE BEST OF McSWEENEY'S
INTERNET TENDENCY

THE BEST OF McSWEENEY'S

INTERNET
TENDENCY

Edited by CHRIS MONKS *and* JOHN WARNER

McSWEENEY'S

M^CSWEENEY'S
SAN FRANCISCO

www.mcsweeneys.net

ISBN 978-1-938073-79-3

Printed in Michigan by Thomson-Shore.

CONTENTS

EDITORS' NOTE

The goal of McSweeney's Internet Tendency, as established by our founder Dave Eggers, has always been modest: publish some brief bit of humorous entertainment on a weekdaily basis.

We've been doing this for fifteen years now, which is several millennia in internet time. Along the way we have achieved modest successes, from cornering the market on the Death Star's trash compactor analysis to establishing just when the yearly decorative gourd season begins.

It was a very difficult task to choose the "best." The book could be five times this length. In the end, we've selected the pieces that strike us as the best representatives for what we've tried to do on our virtual pages for these last fifteen years. We have included our most read articles, but some of your favorites may be missing, for which we apologize. There might even be some fresh discoveries you haven't seen before, which sounds kind of exciting. Some of you might not even know what McSweeney's Internet Tendency is, but have bought the book anyway, which is some strange shit indeed.

In any case, we hope you enjoy, and please remember that there's more where these came from. We don't have plans to stop anytime soon.

Sincerely,
Chris Monks
John Warner
McSweeney's Internet Tendency Editors 2003–2013

I REGRET TO INFORM YOU THAT MY WEDDING TO CAPTAIN VON TRAPP HAS BEEN CANCELED.

by MELINDA TAUB

Dear friends, family, and Austrian nobility,

Captain von Trapp and I are very sorry to inform you that we no longer plan to wed. We offer our deepest apologies to those of you who have already made plans to travel to Salzburg this summer.

Those of you on the Captain's side of the guest list are probably aware of the reason for the change of plans. I'm sure by now you have received that charming "Save the date!" card in the shape of a mountain goat from the Captain and his new fiancée, Maria.

I must confess to being rather blindsided by the end of our relationship. It seems Captain von Trapp and I misunderstood each other. I assumed he was looking for a wife of taste and sophistication, who was a dead ringer for Tippi Hedren; instead he wanted to marry a curtain-wearing religious fanatic who shouts every word she says.

But I don't want you to be angry at him. We are all adults here. "But Baroness," so many of my friends have said, "you must be devastated.

You yourself are fabulously wealthy, so you cannot have wanted the Captain for his money— you must have truly loved him." It's true. But so, I am sure, does his new fiancée, his children's nanny. Her wardrobe is made of curtains. She's definitely not a gold digger or anything.

I'm sorry. That was crude of me. She seems like a lovely person, and she and the children have a great deal in common.

A great, great, great deal.

Since I will no longer be a part of their lives, I do hope you will all keep an eye on the Captain's children. I am not terribly maternal but I was very fond of them in my own way and I must admit I am worried what will become of them now that I have gone. I had planned to send them to boarding school, since their education at the moment seems to consist mostly of marching around Salzburg singing scales. I think it would have been particularly helpful for the eldest daughter, who seems intent on losing her virginity to the mailman.

Please, friends, don't worry about me. While I was a bit startled to be thrown aside for someone who flunked out of nun school, I assure you that I will be fine, and my main pursuits in life shall continue to be martinis, bon mots, and looking fabulous. You'll also be glad to know I have retained custody of the Captain's hard-drinking gay friend, Max. Anyone who gets tired of sing-alongs should feel free to look us up.

Again, my deepest apologies for this disruption to your plans. I am currently sorting through the wedding gifts we've already received and I will send them back as soon as possible. The Captain would help, but he is busy learning to play a song about cuckoo clocks on his guitar.

Sincerely,
Baroness Elsa Schraeder

WHOOPS.

by MIKE SACKS

To: All Staff
9:12 AM
Subject: Whoops, Sorry About That Last E-mail!

I'd just like to apologize for the last e-mail, which I sent to "All Staff."
I meant to send it to my friend Alex Stafford. It was a mistake. Sorry.

- - - -

To: All Staff
10:14 AM
Subject: Clarification on Apology E-mail!

I want to apologize for not being entirely clear in my last e-mail. Let me
try to be more specific: Originally, I was attempting to send my friend
Alex Stafford (not All Staff) an e-mail on horses and how I've always liked
to watch horses run. I then made a leap into the realm of the imaginary.
Again, I do apologize.

- - - -

To: All Staff
11:01 AM
Subject: re: what the fuck?!

Wow. Today just ain't my day! I've been told that I have more
"explaining" to do, re: "the realm of the imaginary." So here goes:
I probably should have told you that for the past two years, give or take
a few months, I've imagined myself as a talking horse and that, as this
talking horse, I've ruled a fantasy kingdom populated by you guys, my
co-workers. The twenty-seven images I included in the first e-mail are, in
fact, Photoshop montages, not actual photos. Carry on!

- - - -

To: All Staff
12:20 PM
Subject: re: You Have More Explaining to Do About Those Images!

There are days and there are days! Perhaps I'm not expressing myself as
well as I should. I guess that's why I'm in accounting and not PR! Okay,
let's start from the very beginning. In this imaginary world I've created,
I'm a talking horse. Simple. You guys are my servants. All of you have
kept your real names, but your "imaginary" selves have taken on new
roles in my fantasy land. A quick example:

"Mary Jenkins" from benefits is a fair maiden who was born in a stable
and grew up to fall in love with "Chris Topp" from payroll, who works
as a candlemaker and sleeps behind the bar in the tavern run by "Wayne

Harris" from the mail room, who is secretly seeing "April Kelly" from office services, who works as my "horse girl" and soaps me down every night before I sleep on my bed of hay. Is this making more sense? For the record, all Photoshop images are a combination of photos found on the internet and your headshots from the company directory. Steve, I'm about ready for lunch if you are.

- - - -

To: All Staff
1:23 PM
Subject: re: I Feel Violated!!!

Imagine my surprise to return from lunch only to find hundreds of e-mails in the ol' inbox! Seems that quite a few of you have additional questions concerning the roles that each of you play within my magical fantasy land. Sigh. It's really quite simple:

"Hope Marks" from the nurse's office refuses to sleep with "Darryl Russell" from security because Darryl is a centaur (see image #6) and Hope is a unicorn (image #3). "Kathryn Haynes" from marketing has caught wind of this because she was born with oversize ears (image #14) and can hear literally everything. She also tends to walk around the village nude (image #8) and sleep with anyone who happens to be available; in one instance, she cavorts with "Jamie Devine" from payroll by the banks of a river, as "Betsy Schneider" and "Krista Stark" from the cafeteria look on in wonder (image #7). I also look on in wonder (images #4 and #5).

In another instance, "Katy Devine" from special projects climbs to the top of the bell tower that's located on my castle and makes love to "Doug Benson" from security, as "Jessica McNally" from the nurse's office braids my tail in a most tender fashion (image #11). She is not wearing a top (image #12) or a bottom (image #13).

Meanwhile, "Alexis Weber" from the front office is an angry dwarf in need of gold. He has just taken on an assignment to kill "Bob Simmons" from purchasing, but only after he has promised "Marina DelGado" from human resources that he will turn her into a good witch by way of a magical spell. This magical spell consists of having sex with a complete stranger ("Mitch Morton," also from human resources) while riding a white mare, ass-back and fancy-free, across a great plain (image #9). The horse, if you haven't already guessed, is me (image #1). In the background, if you look closely enough, you can just make out "Joe Griggs" from janitorial looking on in wonder (image #2).

Whew! Done! By the way, anyone have the forms for the Milner project? I *really* need them by this afternoon. Thanks!

- - - -

To: All Staff
3:12 PM
Subject: re: you're sick!

Holy cripes! Sometimes I wonder if anyone besides me gets any work done around here! I step away from my desk for two seconds and I come back to discover that a thousand more questions have been posed! Don't get me wrong: I think it's super that all of you are taking an active interest in my fantasy kingdom, but my goodness! So let me just tie up one loose end and let me do it real, real quick, because I've just been notified that I've been fired:

Yes, that is you, "Samantha Rymer" from expenses, standing next to a razzleberry bush in image #15. And yes, Samantha, that is indeed a crown of doves perched atop your head, and no, Samantha, those are not your real breasts (images #16–27).

Everyone up to date? I'm really gonna miss all of you! I feel we've become especially close over these past two years! And that even goes for "Marina the Good Witch" from human resources! I honestly did not know that "good witches" could get so angry! LOL!

Your Imaginary Leader Who's Now Waving Goodbye as
Kathy from Security Hangs On Tightly and Rides Him
(please see attached image),
Mike the Talking Horse

IT'S DECORATIVE GOURD SEASON, MOTHERFUCKERS.

by COLIN NISSAN

I don't know about you, but I can't wait to get my hands on some fucking gourds and arrange them in a horn-shaped basket on my dining room table. That shit is going to look so seasonal. I'm about to head up to the attic right now to find that wicker fucker, dust it off, and jam it with an insanely ornate assortment of shellacked vegetables. When my guests come over it's gonna be like, BLAMMO! Check out my shellacked decorative vegetables, assholes. Guess what season it is—fucking fall. There's a nip in the air and my house is full of mutant fucking squash.

I may even throw some multicolored leaves into the mix, all haphazard like a crisp October breeze just blew through and fucked that shit up. Then I'm going to get to work on making a beautiful fucking gourd necklace for myself. People are going to be like, "Aren't those gourds straining your neck?" And I'm just going to thread another gourd onto my necklace without breaking their gaze and quietly reply, "It's fall, fuckfaces. You're either ready to reap this freaky-assed harvest or you're not."

Carving orange pumpkins sounds like a pretty fitting way to ring in the season. You know what else does? Performing an all-gourd reenactment of an episode of *Diff'rent Strokes*—specifically the one when Arnold and Dudley experience a disturbing brush with sexual molestation. Well, this shit just got real, didn't it? Felonies and gourds have one very important commonality: they're both extremely fucking real. Sorry if that's upsetting, but I'm not doing you any favors by shielding you from this anymore.

The next thing I'm going to do is carve one of the longer gourds into a perfect replica of the *Mayflower* as a shout-out to our Pilgrim forefathers. Then I'm going to do lines of blow off its hull with a hooker. Why? Because it's not summer, it's not winter, and it's not spring. Grab a calendar and pull your fucking heads out of your asses; it's fall, fuckers.

Have you ever been in an Italian deli with salamis hanging from their ceiling? Well then you're going to fucking love my house. Just look where you're walking or you'll get KO'd by the gauntlet of misshapen, zucchini-descendant bastards swinging from above. And when you do, you're going to hear a very loud, very stereotypical Italian laugh coming from me. Consider yourself warned.

For now, all I plan to do is to throw on a flannel shirt, some tattered overalls, and a floppy fucking hat and stand in the middle of a cornfield for a few days. The first crow that tries to land on me is going to get his avian ass bitch-slapped all the way back to summer.

Welcome to autumn, fuckheads!

TRIPADVISOR.COM REVIEWS: JEKYLL & HYDE B&B.

by KATE HAHN

"A real gem"

Five out of five stars! Host Jekyll so friendly and accommodating. (Did not meet partner Hyde.) Highly recommended. Just what a British B&B should be! Jekyll showed us his charming basement laboratory (yes—pronounced it that oh-so-English way!), where he's working on "experiments." Cute! Probably where he cooks up the amazing home-made jam. Three kinds at breakfast. One was quince!

"Almost perfect"

Agree, Jekyll stellar. But be aware: delicate situation with Hyde due to physical handicaps—limping, speech impediment. But loved his enthusiasm when it came to killing spider in our room at midnight! Not to mention brute strength with luggage. Only two kinds of jam (black currant, gooseberry) but tasty.

"Gem? Not even jam!"

Did we stay at same place as above posters? Did not meet Jekyll, only Hyde. Limp and slur, probably from drinking! Actually leered at my wife and played grabby hands. No vacancy elsewhere or would have left. Lots of noise—walls paper-thin ... heard moaning and groaning coming from downstairs all night ... Jam sounds nice. Barely had toast.

"Highs, but more lows"

Earlier post made us slightly apprehensive, since we had already made our reservations and sent deposit ... Relieved when met at front door by Jekyll. Polite but pale and shaking visibly. Why didn't anyone mention his smoking? Place reeked and he lit one after the other. Kindly set up croquet wickets for us in garden, then went off into woods—minutes later, Hyde loped out of the trees with rabbit that he had obviously killed with bare hands. Could not finish croquet game after that. Is this the famous British eccentricity? Checked out before breakfast, so not sure of jam situation.

"Won't go BACK"

Stayed on a whim—wish I had read posts before. Not his fault, but Jekyll had really bad back spasm while pouring tea in morning. Suddenly hunched forward and could not stand up again. Bared teeth in pained grimace. Hands frozen in clawlike shape. He kept calling, "Hyde!," who never showed up to help. Awkward when we tried to check out, because Jekyll could not run our credit card with fingers stuck in claw position.

"Scary dude"

Hyde answered door, eating jam (brambleberry?) straight from the jar with his fingers. Said Jekyll was "gone forever." Dirty dishes on table. Broken glass beaker on floor. We are two girls traveling alone. Felt uncomfortable. Did not check in.

"hEP me"

Writing from compter at b&b. RUN. DO NOT OCME he … hep …

"Closed"

Not sure about above post. Flag? Curious, so walked past one evening on way back to our B/B. Met guy on porch who said he was Jekyll's lawyer, and that B/B closed indefinitely and no one home. But, as walking away, we saw light in basement window and hunched figure moving around. Maybe exterminators? Or Jekyll getting back in swing of things to make more jam? I'll put in a request for some damson plum!

ON THE IMPLAUSIBILITY OF THE DEATH STAR'S TRASH COMPACTOR.

by J. M. TYREE

I maintain that the trash compactor onboard the Death Star in *Star Wars* is implausible, unworkable, and moreover, inefficient.

The Trash Compactor Debate turns on whether the Death Star ejects its trash into space. I, for one, believe it does. Though we never see the Death Star ejecting its trash, we do see another Empire ship, the so-called Star Destroyer, ejecting its trash into space. I therefore see no reason to suspect that Empire protocol dictating that trash be ejected into space would not apply equally to all Empire spacecraft, including the Death Star.

The Death Star clearly has a garbage-disposal problem. Given its size and massive personnel, the amount of waste it generates—discarded food, broken equipment, excrement, and the like—boggles the imagination. That said, I just cannot fathom how an organization as ruthless and efficiently run as the Empire would have signed off on such a dangerous, unsanitary, and shoddy garbage-disposal system as the one depicted in the movie.

Here are the problems, as I can ascertain them, with the Death Star's garbage-disposal system:

1. Ignoring the question of how Princess Leia could possibly know where the trash compactor is, or that the vent she blasts open leads to a good hiding place for the rescue crew, why are there vents leading down there at all? Would not vents leading into any garbage-disposal system allow the fetid smell of rotting garbage, spores, molds, etc., to seep up into the rest of the Death Star? Would not it have been more prudent for the designers of the Death Star to opt for a closed system, like a septic tank?

2. Why do both walls of the trash compactor move toward each other, rather than employing a one-movable-wall system that would thus rely on the anchored stability, to say nothing of the strength, of the other, non-moving wall, to crush trash more effectively?

3. Why does the trash compactor compact trash so slowly, and with such difficulty, once the resistance of a thin metal rod is introduced? Surely metal Death Star pieces are one of the main items of trash in need of compacting. It thus stands to reason that the trash compactor should have been better designed to handle the problem of a skinny piece of metal. (And while I hate to be the sort of person who says I told you so, I'd be remiss if I didn't point out that a one-movable-wall system would have improved performance.)

4. Why does the trash compactor only compact trash sideways? Once ejected into space, wouldn't the flattened, living-room-sized, and extremely solid panes of trash that result from such a primitive, unidirectional trash compactor pose serious hazards for Empire starships in the vicinity?

5. And what of the creature that lives in the trash compactor? Presumably, the creature survives because the moving walls do not extend all the way to the floor of the room, where the liquid is. After all, if the walls reached the floor, the creature would be killed each time trash is compacted. The design employed on the Death Star must allow the organic trash to filter down to the bottom, where the parasitic worm-creature devours it. But what happens when heavier pieces of nonorganic trash fall down there? Would such trash not get wedged under the doors, causing them to malfunction? Do stormtroopers have to confront the creature each time they retrieve pieces of uncompacted trash?

6. Why not have separate systems for organic and inorganic waste, thus allowing full compaction of the inorganics and a closed sanitary system for the organics?

7. Why does the Empire care, anyway, about reducing its organic-garbage output? Are we to believe that the architects of the Death Star, a group of individuals bent on controlling the entire known universe, are also concerned about environmental issues? Would organic garbage rot in space? So what? Furthermore, why has the Empire gone to the trouble of acquiring a frightening parasitic worm-creature and having it eat all organic trash, especially given the aforementioned flaws in the design of the compactor and overall maintenance hassles?

8. Personally, were it up to me, I would have designed special garbage ships instead of employing a crude, cumbersome, and inefficient (to say nothing of unsanitary) compactor-worm combo to deal with the trash.

9. If the Empire insists on ejecting trash into space, why do they bother compacting it? Space is infinite, is it not? In such an environment, it hardly matters what size the trash is. In fact, a persuasive argument can be made that it's actually better for the trash to take up more space, so that it appears on radar systems as something for Empire ships to avoid. Compacted trash creates smaller chunks of harder trash that would undoubtedly cause serious damage to Empire starships. And needless to say, damage to starships would, in turn, create yet more hassles and headaches for the Empire.

Please understand, gentle reader, I am all for creating hassles and headaches for the Empire. I just doubt that the Empire would have created so many for itself. QED.

IN WHICH I FIX MY GIRLFRIEND'S GRANDPARENTS' WI-FI AND AM HAILED AS A CONQUERING HERO.

by MIKE LACHER

Lo, in the twilight days of the second year of the second decade of the third millennium did a great darkness descend over the wireless internet connectivity of the people of 276 Ferndale Street in the North-Central lands of Iowa. For many years, the gentlefolk of these lands basked in a wireless network overflowing with speed and ample internet, flowing like a river into their Compaq Presario. Many happy days did the people spend checking Hotmail and reading USAToday.com.

But then one gray morning did Internet Explorer 6 no longer load The Google. Refresh was clicked, again and again, but still did Internet Explorer 6 not load The Google. Perhaps The Google was broken, the people thought, but then The Yahoo too did not load. Nor did Hotmail. Nor USAToday.com. The land was thrown into panic. Internet Explorer 6 was minimized then maximized. The Compaq Presario was unplugged then plugged back in. The old mouse was brought out and plugged in beside the new mouse. Still, The Google did not load.

Some in the kingdom thought the cause of the darkness must be the Router. Little was known of the Router; legend told it had been installed behind the recliner long ago by a shadowy organization known as Comcast. Others in the kingdom believed it was brought by a distant cousin many feasts ago. Concluding the trouble must lie deep within the microchips, the people of 276 Ferndale Street did despair and resign themselves to defeat.

But with the dawn of the feast of Christmas did a beacon of hope manifest itself upon the inky horizon. Riding in upon a teal Ford Focus came a great warrior, a suitor of the gentlefolks' granddaughter. Word had spread through the kingdom that this warrior worked with computers and perhaps even knew the true nature of the Router.

The people did beseech the warrior to aid them. They were a simple people, capable only of rewarding him with gratitude and a larger-than-normal serving of Jell-O salad. The warrior considered the possible battles before him. While others may have shirked the duties, forcing the good people of Ferndale Street to prostrate themselves before the tyrants of Comcast, Linksys, and Geek Squad, the warrior could not chill his heart to these depths. He accepted the quest and strode bravely across the beige shag carpet of the living room.

Deep, deep behind the recliner did the warrior crawl, over great mountains of *National Geographic* magazines and deep chasms of *TV Guides*. At last he reached a gnarled thicket of cords, a terrifying knot of gray and white and black and blue threatening to ensnare all who ventured further. The warrior charged ahead. Weaker men would have lost their minds in the madness: telephone cords plugged into Ethernet jacks, AC adapters plugged into phone jacks, a lone VGA cable wrapped in a firm knot around an Ethernet cord. But the warrior bested the thicket, ripping away the vestigial cords and swiftly untangling the deadly trap.

And at last the warrior arrived at the Router. It was a dusty black box with an array of shimmering green lights, blinking on and off, as if to taunt him to come any further. The warrior swiftly maneuvered to the rear of the router and verified what he had feared, what he had heard whispered in his ear from spirits beyond: all the cords were securely in place.

The warrior closed his eyes, summoning the power of his ancestors, long departed but watchful still. And then with the echoing beep of his digital watch, he moved with deadly speed, wrapping his battle-hardened hands around the power cord at the back of the Router.

Gripping it tightly, he pulled with all his force, dislodging the cord from the Router. The heavens roared. The Earth wailed. The green lights turned off. Silently the warrior counted. One. Two. Three. And just as swiftly, the warrior plugged the cord back into the Router. Great crashes of blood-red lightning boomed overhead. Murders of crows blackened the skies. The POWER light came on solid green. The seas rolled. The WLAN light blinked on. The forests ignited. A dark fog rolled over the land and suddenly all was silent. The warrior stared at the INTERNET light, waiting, waiting. And then, as the world around him seemed all but dead, the INTERNET light began to blink.

The warrior darted out back over the mountains of *National Geographic* magazines and made haste to the Compaq Presario. He woke up Windows XP from sleep mode and deftly defeated twelve notifications to update Norton AntiVirus. With a resounding click he opened Internet Explorer 6 and gazed deep into its depths, past The Yahoo toolbar, the MSN toolbar, the Ask.com toolbar, and the AOL toolbar. And then did he see, at long last, that The Google did load.

And so the good people of the kingdom were delighted and did heap laurels and Jell-O salad at the warrior's feet, for now again they could have their Hotmail as the wireless internet did flow freely to their Compaq Presario. The warrior ate his Jell-O salad, thanked the gentlefolk, and then went to the basement because the TiVo was doing something weird with the VCR.

Response to *On the Implausibility of the*
Death Star's Trash Compactor #1

———— ∞∞∞ ————

From: Seth Fisher
Date: Thu, Nov 8, 2012
Re: Plausible explanations for the Death Star Compaction
System

Just trying to play Devil's Advocate. I thoroughly enjoyed
the read:

1. Why are there vents leading down there at all?

   It's not large enough to serve the entire space station.
   That room probably serves just a few levels, and to make
   things easy there are chutes at each level you can toss the
   trash into. Perhaps only the prison level's is vented?

2. Why do both walls of the trash compactor move toward
   each other?

   You're thinking in terms of energy efficiency. The Death
   Star runs off of a seemingly limitless energy source at
   its core. Plus, we don't know the mechanism. If it were
   hydraulics or pneumatics, then yes, you're doubling the
   parts and it doesn't make sense. What if instead, though,
   the walls are part of a compression system that doubles as
   deck ventilation? As the airtight walls move toward each
   other, you create a vacuum on either side that can suck
   in air through vents (i.e., the one on the prison deck that

is no longer dumping directly into the trash). The two sides then serve to air out different parts of that level.

3. Why does the trash compactor compact trash so slowly, and with such difficulty, once the resistance of a thin metal rod is introduced?

I don't think the rod did anything to slow it. I think it compacts slower as resistance builds with all the other stuff in there and the metal rod is just the work of a farmboy who doesn't understand physics. You'll note the highly educated Senator/Princess's plan is "climb on top of it." Perhaps the rod isn't meant to slow the compaction, but to serve as a ladder the heroes could use to climb upward as the walls got closer?

4. Why does the trash compactor only compact trash sideways?

You're expecting the trash to be ejected into space. For a starship, that makes sense, but the Death Star spends much of its time in a small orbit, thus large amounts of detritus buildup is unwise. More likely, the trash is vented inward into the station's power source and destroyed. Making it into flat sheets would allow the system to have very good control of the rate at which the matter is ejected into the power source—or, if they recycle the material (which is mostly metal), good control over the rate of slag to be melted.

5. And what of the creature that lives in the trash compactor?

The creature probably does indeed live off the organic matter, probably getting more than enough with the floating stuff that it doesn't leave the surface except to escape. You'll note it has developed a very keen sense of when the trash is about to be compacted, so keen that it lets a big meal (Luke) go immediately. I would guess the creature is serpentine and that it has found a drain. Also, I would guess most ships have these and plan safe pipes for them.

6. Why not have separate systems for organic and inorganic waste, thus allowing full compaction of the inorganics and a closed sanitary system for the organics?

Again, this is more evidence for incineration, not expulsion into space.

7. Why has the Empire gone to the trouble of acquiring a frightening parasitic worm-creature and having it eat all organic trash?

Back to the worm. I would bet it evolved over millenia in non–space trash compaction systems. Perhaps because its ancestors were so useful, it is considered simple good luck to have one on board any deep-space vessel, just as a ship without rats in the Age of Sail was cast darkly. A more plausible explanation is that the creature can naturally break down more than just human waste. Like, maybe it eats lubricant oils that would otherwise not allow the slag sheets to remain cohesive … or some sort of corrosive acid that would hasten the breakdown of their septic systems.

8. Personally, were it up to me, I would have designed special garbage ships instead of employing a crude, cumbersome, and inefficient (to say nothing of unsanitary) compactor-worm combo to deal with the trash.

That is the least efficient way to deal with it! Just send the shit to the core and be done with it—save the ships for dogfighting X-Wings.

9. If the Empire insists on ejecting trash into space, why do they bother compacting it?

I'm convinced they incinerate it.

10. Please understand, gentle reader, I am all for creating hassles and headaches for the Empire. I just doubt that the Empire would have created so many for itself. QED.

You obviously don't have much experience with totalitarian governments and their staggering inefficiencies. It's not too far-fetched to imagine in such a government that the dude who designed a superfluous compaction-ejection system with twice the necessary parts and put a worm in it was the nephew of a high-ranking official. Traveling faster than light, however ... that's just total science fiction.
—Seth

WHAT I WOULD BE THINKING ABOUT IF I WERE BILLY JOEL DRIVING TOWARD A HOLIDAY PARTY WHERE I KNEW THERE WAS GOING TO BE A PIANO.

by MICHAEL IAN BLACK

I'm not doing it. I'm just not. I know I say the same thing every year, but this time I mean it—I am not playing it this year. Seriously, how many times can I possibly be expected to play that stupid song? I bet if you counted the number of times I've played it over the years, it probably adds up to, like, a jillion. I'm not even exaggerating. One jillion times. Well, not this year.

This year, I'm just going to say, "Sorry, folks, I'm only playing holiday songs tonight." Yeah, that's a good plan. That's definitely what I'm going to do, and if they don't like it, tough cookies. It'll just be tough cookies for them.

But I know exactly what'll happen. I'll sit down, play a few holiday songs, and then some drunk jerk will yell out, "'Piano Man,'" and everybody will start clapping, and I'll look like a real asshole if I don't play it.

I wonder if they'll have shrimp cocktail.

Now that I think of it, it's always Bob Schimke who yells out, "'Piano Man.'" He does it every year. He gets a couple of Scotches in that fat gut of his, and then it's, "Hey, Billy, play 'Piano Man'!" That guy is such a dick. He thinks he's such a big shot because he manages that stupid hedge fund. Big deal. He thinks because he used to play quarterback for Amherst that everybody should give a shit. I don't. Who cares about you and your stupid hedge fund, Bob? That's what I should say to him this year. I really should. I should just march right up to him and say, "Who cares about your stupid hedge fund, you dick?" Let's just see what Mr. Quarterback has to say about that. And I know he made a pass at Christie that time. She probably liked it—that's probably why she denied it even happened.

I'm such a loser.

Why do I even go to these parties? I mean, honestly, how many times do I need to see Trish and Steve and Lily and that creepy doctor husband of hers and all their rich Long Island friends? Although that Greenstein girl is nice. Maybe she'll be there. What's her name—Alison?

What if Alison asks me to play "Piano Man"? Then what? I've got to stick to my guns, that's what. I'll simply say, "Some other time." Yeah, that's good. Kind of like we're making a date or something. And then at the end of the night when we're all getting our coats, I'll turn to her and say something like, "So when do you want to get together and hear 'Piano Man'?" Oh man, that's really good. That's so smooth. After all, how is she going to say no? She's the one who asked to hear it in the first place! Oh man, Billy, that is just perfect.

Maybe she'll say something like, "How about right now?" Yeah. And maybe we'll leave together. I can drive her back to my place and I can play her the stupid song and then maybe we'll do it. I'd really like to do it with that Greenstein girl. How awesome would that be? Me leaving with Alison on my arm and Bob's big fat stupid face watching us go. That would be too rich. I'd be real nonchalant about it, too—"See you later, Bob."

Who am I kidding? She'd never go out with me. She was dating that actor for a while. What's his name? Benicio? What kind of name is Benicio? A stupid name, that's what kind. Hi, I'm Benicio. I'm so cool. I'm sooooo cool. I should start going by Billicio. I'm Billicio Del Joelio. I play pianolo.

Sing us a song, you're the piano man ...

Oh great. Now it's in my head. Perfect. Now I have to walk around that stupid party with that stupid song stuck in my head all night.

Amherst sucks at football.

You know what I should do? I should just turn this car around and go home. Just pick up the phone and call them and tell them I ate some bad fish or something. Yeah, that's what I should do. This party's going to suck anyway. By the time I get there, all the shrimp cocktail will probably be gone anyway.

What am I going to do? Go through my entire life avoiding situations where somebody might ask me to play a song? I can't do that. No, Billy, you've just got to grow yourself a sack and take care of business. And if that loudmouth Bob Schimke requests "Piano Man," I just need to look him in the eye and tell him I'd be happy to play it for him just as soon as he goes ahead and fucks himself.

Who am I kidding? Of course I'm going to play it. I always play it. Probably the only reason half the people at that party even show up is to hear me play "Piano Man." They probably don't even like me. Not really. They just want to tell all their friends that Billy came and played "Piano Man." Again. Like I'm the loser who's dying to play it. Whatever.

Fine. I'll do it, but not because they want me to, but because I want me to. I'm not even going to wait for them to ask. I'm going to march right in there and play the song and that'll be that. I'm not even going to take off my coat first. Yeah. Let's see what Bob has to say about that. I might even play it twice.

COVERING TEEN WOLF:
ONE COACH'S GUIDE.

by PASHA MALLA

Used to be, the key to beating Teen Wolf's Beavers was just to play them on any night there wasn't a full moon. We were unlucky one season in that we met them twenty-eight days apart, both times in their barn, and Teen Wolf destroyed us—sixty-four points in the first game, then a quadruple-double in the second, with fourteen blocked shots and twenty-five steals. Our third matchup, though, we were fortunate enough to have a 76 percent waxing gibbous, so it was regular Scott Howard, who turned the ball over twice before fouling out, scoreless, in eight minutes of play. These days, however, it seems the guy can change over whenever he wants, which poses a real problem to opposing coaches. What follows is the best strategy my staff and I have come up with to limit Teen Wolf's effectiveness on the court. While admittedly far from foolproof, it will, hopefully, prove useful to your team. We're all in this together, folks.

To begin, you're going to have to resign yourself to the fact that Teen Wolf is probably going to drop at least fifty points. That might seem like a lot, but, unfortunately, it's just the way the ball bounces. As coach, you need to recognize that your job isn't to do the impossible; you're not going to stop Teen Wolf entirely, but you can try to contain him by making him play your team's style of basketball. Discipline and defensive fundamentals help: nose on the ball, feet moving, channeling him into traps—careful with those, though. Soon as Teen Wolf gets two guys on him, he tends to find the open man. He's a heads-up ballplayer with great court sense, so if you're going to bring a trapping zone against Teen Wolf, make sure you have solid weak-side rotation and your defenders are communicating.

Of course, that's only if he feels like passing. Teen Wolf gets scrappy once you put the pressure on, and he's a great ball handler with a low-to-the-ground style reminiscent of Pistol Pete or a young Isiah Thomas. Add to his skill and quickness those gigantic, hirsute paws, and you're up against one hell of a dribbler. We've tried giving Teen Wolf a step, respecting his speed, but we've found that if our guys slack off him, he'll generally hit the open jumper—or else take off from wherever he's standing on the court, sail over everyone's heads, and finish with one of those dunks where he ends up sitting on the top of the backboard, howling, feet dangling down through the hoop.

While you're welcome to try it, my feeling is that man-to-man defense simply isn't an option. Some teams like to play a box-and-one, which generally works well against most lycanthropes. With Teen Wolf, though, you have to be careful. He'll just stand baying by the sideline while the rest of the Beavers run four-on-four. Then, at a signal from Coach Finstock, Teen Wolf will come screaming down the lane, fur bristling and fangs bared, for the alley-oop. (And with him having what's rumored to be a seventy-eight-inch standing vertical leap, rest assured he's even more difficult to stop once he gets up in the air.) I've heard of coaches dealing with this by putting a sniper in the crowd with a box of silver bullets and a hunting rifle. We tried it once, back when Teen Wolf was only a freshman: the shooter missed, and when the cops showed up and cleared the gym we were forced to default.

So, I bet you're wondering: if it's impossible to cover him through conventional defenses, what can we do? Here's the key: Teen Wolf doesn't get along with his teammates. While he's certainly got the individual skills to dominate most games, I'd have to struggle to think of ever seeing a more selfish player in my twenty-eight years of coaching. He tends to alienate his fellow Beavers by doing things like stealing the ball off them, or stealing their girlfriends, and their resentment is easy for opposing teams to exploit. Sympathy seems to work well; get your players to say stuff like, "Man, sure sucks playing with Teen Wolf," or "I'd hate to have a guy like Teen Wolf on my team," and you'll be surprised how quickly the Beavers' team defense will start to open up.

Another trick is to keep on the officials about aggressive play. Granted, most refs are pretty scared to call anything on Teen Wolf, what with the risk of being devoured in the parking lot after the game. Still, it's hard to ignore someone being gouged by lupine talons, especially if the player's entrails are exposed. Coach Finstock hates sitting Teen Wolf, but if his star picks up three fouls early, there won't be any other option. Just make sure to tell your guys to resist taunting Teen Wolf while he's on the bench; it only makes him angrier, and with that anger comes frightening strength.

Finally, keep in mind that beneath all that fur, Teen Wolf is only human—or half human, whatever—with weaknesses, just like any of us. And as a hormonally imbalanced, eternally cursed teenager, he's particularly fragile. For one thing, at just under 70 percent, Teen Wolf's free-throw shooting is comparatively weak; if you've got a kid on your team brave or crazy enough to knock Teen Wolf down with a hard foul, encourage it. Make him earn his points at the line. "Hack-a-Wolf" brought us within ten of the Beavers during last year's playoffs—that is, until Teen Wolf dunked eight consecutive trips down the floor from the three-point line, putting the lead out of reach.

Okay, that's pretty much all I've got. As I mentioned earlier, defending Teen Wolf isn't an exact science, and you're more than welcome to alter these tactics as befits your own ball club. I hope that between us we can keep the lines of communication open and continue to share strategies that seem to work. My feeling is that there's no team that is completely unbeatable, even if their star transforms into a werewolf before every game. Oh, and if you come up with some way of preventing Teen Wolf from jumping up and catching your team's shots, I'd be particularly interested in hearing it.

Thanks, and best of luck.

HELLO STRANGER ON THE STREET, COULD YOU PLEASE TELL ME HOW TO TAKE CARE OF MY BABY?

by WENDY MOLYNEUX

Oh, hello, person I have never met before! I am so glad you ran up to me on this street where I am walking with my baby. You did not scare me at all with your very loud voice and the way you grabbed my arm! In fact, I am super relieved because I have a series of questions about my baby that I hope you can answer, and I am going to ask them because I know you would never ever offer me unsolicited advice.

First of all, should he be sleeping, ever? If so, should it be at night? Should I keep him in a bassinet or crib or should I let him just sleep in the yard, or the toaster? And when he sleeps, should I just let him sleep as long as he wants, or should I wake him up every fifteen minutes or so for a "baby party" where I give him hard candies and play loud music? Being a new parent is confusing, and there aren't any books or internets about it, that's why I have to rely on kind strangers like you.

Yes, he IS crying, isn't he? You are right. He's probably hungry. Should I feed him? And if so, where do I put the food? His eyeball? His butt? What kinds of cuts of meat do babies like? Should I not give him hot peppers? How much salt is too much, and when can I expect him to use a knife? If he spits up, should I have him put to sleep? There are just so many things I need to know, and that is why I rely on total strangers like you who happen to be experts on child care.

Oh, that rash on his face? Well, the doctor told me that it was just baby acne that would go away in a few weeks and that it's incredibly common. But I really appreciate you pointing it out! I hadn't looked at his face yet! Probably because I couldn't tell which part of the baby was the face. Is his elbow his face? Is his onesie his face? Thank you!

Oh nice lady, you are probably right! I should definitely cover his face always so he doesn't get sun on it. If he is exposed to the sun for even one moment, even as I am simply walking from the mechanic to a coffee shop where I have to unexpectedly stop to feed him because my car broke down, he will probably immediately get sun disease or burst into flames.

I am so glad you stopped me! I can't wait to hear more about your grandchildren. What cuts of meat do they like? Were they ever babies, or did they start out as cats or dogs? And what did you start out as? A regular human being who was generally respectful to others or a nosy monster who is about to get kicked in the neck by a woman with a BabyBjörn on her chest? What? No! Don't walk away! Please! We were just getting started! I have so many more questions! Am I still pregnant after the baby came out? Can they play with tigers? Aaaaaaaaaaaaaaaaaagh! When is it okay for him to go upside down in his car seat!?!

A POST-GENDER-NORMATIVE MAN TRIES TO PICK UP A WOMAN AT A BAR.

by JESSE EISENBERG

Hey, how's it going? Mind if I sidle up? I saw you over here sitting alone and I thought, That's fine. A woman should be able to self-sustain. In fact a lot of women are choosing to stay alone, what with advances in salary equitability and maternity extensions, and I think it's an important and compelling trend.

I noticed that you were about to finish your drink and I was wondering if I could possibly watch you purchase another one. And, at the risk of being forward, if you could possibly purchase one for me.

What do you do? And before you answer, I'm not looking for a necessarily work-related response. I don't think we have to be defined by our industrial pursuits, especially when they're antiquated and hetero-normative. I curse my mother, who is an otherwise lovely human person, for not buying me an Easy-Bake Oven when I was younger. I grew up idolizing male thugs like Neil Armstrong and Jimmy Carter. And, yes, I work at ESPN, but I spend more time being spiritual and overcoming adversity, for example, than I do working for some faceless corporation.

And if I were to find a mate, be it you or someone else here tonight, I would be more than happy to tell the proverbial "man" that I quit so I can raise our offspring with gender-neutral hobbies, while my biologically female partner continues to pursue her interests, be they industrial, recreational, or yes, even sexual, with another mate.

So ...

Crazy news about the first female African head of state and Liberia's sitting president, Ellen Johnson-Sirleaf, huh? Announcing her candidacy for 2011 so soon! Wow. What do you think of her chances? I think she's a shoo-in, but I'm admittedly a bit concerned about Prince Johnson making some last minute strides, especially amongst the Gio people in the Nimba region. I'm thinking of launching a letter writing campaign on behalf of EJ-S or at least cold calling potential Nimba voters over Skype.

Oh, how gauche of me! I've just been chattering away incessantly like some kind of boy or girl who talks a lot. I haven't even properly introduced myself. Although, one often gets the uneasy sense that patriarchy dictates a learned and ultimately damaging order of events with men taking an unearned lead. My name is Terri, with a heart over the *i*, instead of a dot. I have a heart, is what that says, and I'm not afraid to wear it on my sleeve.

So what do you think? Would you like to take me up on my offer for you to buy me that drink?

If you would like to respond, that would be wonderful. Of course, if you would like to continue to sit here silently, staring at me with that powerful gaze, which both breaks gender constructs and also scares me a bit, that would be fine as well.

What's that? I should go fuck myself? I agree! Men should be more self-generative! Thank you for your astute assertion. Why should women exclusively have to bear the burden of childbirth, when men are biologically doomed to fear commitment? It's counterintuitive and socially degrading.

Ahh, that beer is refreshing! Thank you for throwing it in my face on this warm summer evening.

Okay, okay! I'm leaving!

Thank you for your blunt rejection of me. It takes a lot of courage, which you no doubt have in equal measure to any other human. Now, if you'll excuse me, I'm going to the bathroom where I'll cry silently in a stall, questioning my body and texting my mom, but for now, I thank you for your time, which was equal to mine.

LISTEN, KID, THE BIGGEST THING YOU'VE GOT GOING FOR YOU IS YOUR RACK.

by ELLIE KEMPER

Listen, Sandy, you're a nice girl. You've got an okay voice. You seem like you can call the shots. But when all is said and done, the biggest thing you have on your side is your huge rack.

I'm sure you've got brains, too. Hell, we all do. But that's not what counts in this biz. That's not what's gonna make you a star. And I can't make a star out of someone who can't make the cut. Hell, a big rack helps. But it's not gonna make the cut.

We've seen you before, and we like your style. We like your attitude, the sparkle in your eyes, the fight in your face. But you just can't hit those notes. Your ass is too wide, and you can't hit those notes.

I've gotta lotta girls going for this part. Girls who are good. Girls who are stars. And you just ain't on that level yet. You're good, but you're not there. You need to work on a lotta things; you gotta get your chops. The one thing you don't need to work on—the thing that's doing half the work for you—is your giant rack.

Where'd you get that rack, anyhow? Is that from your mom? I don't wanna be too creepy, but those melons look real. Not the fake-boat kind, like the kind I see on some of these broads. Some of those globes you could use as basketballs! Slam dunk! But not yours, Sandy. Yours look like the real thing.

Hey, does your back ever hurt from carrying around those jugs in front? Once, I had to change a tire, only I had to carry the tire almost half a mile from the station to get it back to my wheels. My back was so sore I couldn't sit up straight for days. The thing is, I wonder if you've got the same problem with your rack. That thing is huge, and all on your front. I'm just sitting here, and I'm thinking, and I'm wondering to myself: Doesn't her back hurt from carrying around those enormous ta-tas?

You know what I'd do if you were my girl? I'd take my face and I'd bury it in your mo-mos. I tell you what, if it were my choice, there'd be only one way for me to go—suffocation in your mo-mos. Or if we were in a boxing match, but instead of gloves, you punched with your grapefruits. Smothered by your mo-mos or battered by your grapefruits: either way, you could color me a happy papa.

What's really got me going is, you mentioned you like to go for long jogs around Lakeside Park. So you say that, and I hear that, and I'm thinking, How can she handle that? Aren't your bullets socking you in the face the whole time? I know you've got a harness, but gravity is gravity, kid—and I'm wondering why your cheeks aren't black and blue.

Listen, baby, you're gonna be a star. I want you to be a star. But you just ain't there yet. If you keep working on those notes—and believe me, I told Chi-Chi Fernandez about you; she's gonna help you out, kid—I know you can make it to the big time. I want you to make it to the big time. But for now, the biggest thing you've got is your rack.

AN OVERHEARD CONVERSATION AT THE SUBURBAN NEIGHBORHOOD POOL, IF THE SUBURBAN NEIGHBORHOOD POOL WERE IN DEADWOOD.

by KARI ANNE ROY

MOM 1: Fucking Homeowners Association cocksuckers. Are they so slow in the ass-fucking cerebrum as to not allow a goddamned simple, commonplace, gullet-pleasing peanut-fucking-butter sandwich on the premises of their fucking pool patio?

MOM 2: Fucking power-hungry vulturine twats is what they are, that Homeowners Association you speak of.

MOM 1: I mean, fuck me if I'm gonna take the three angelic fucking spawn of my hooch and force them to hunker their tiny selves down in the back of the sweltering cocksucking Odyssey just to masticate a PB&J and imbibe some goddamned Mott's. Fuck.

MOM 2: Want I should write a letter to the HOA fuckers and invite them to a civil fucking sit-down where we can discuss this fucking asinine and irritating issue face to face?

MOM 1: Fuck no. It wouldn't do any good. I doubt any of the fuckers can read.

MOM 2: Well, shit, Tiffany, let's just divvy up the sandwiches among our sweet fucking runts and see what happens. Hunter's gone all asshole from hunger-induced madness of the brain, already.

MOM 1: Indeed, Jennifer. Let's buck the fucking antiquated "system" of HOA whores trying to prevent ants and the like from invading the fucking pool area. Ants I can abso-fucking-lutely deal with. Insane children? Jesus Christ on a bike, that shit is impossible to manage.

MOM 2: KIDS! FUCKING LUNCHTIME!

MOM 1: DON'T FORGET TO WASH YOUR GODDAMNED HANDS!

BACK FROM YET ANOTHER GLOBETROTTING ADVENTURE, INDIANA JONES CHECKS HIS MAIL AND DISCOVERS THAT HIS BID FOR TENURE HAS BEEN DENIED.

by ANDY BRYAN

January 22, 1939

Assistant Professor Henry "Indiana" Jones Jr.
Department of Anthropology
Chapman Hall 227B
Marshall College

Dr. Jones:

As chairman of the Committee on Promotion and Tenure, I regret to inform you that your recent application for tenure has been denied by a vote of six to one. Following past policies and procedures, proceedings from the committee's deliberations that were pertinent to our decision have been summarized below according to the assessment criteria.

DEMONSTRATES SUITABLE EXPERIENCE AND
EXPERTISE IN CHOSEN FIELD:

The committee concurred that Dr. Jones does seem to possess a nearly superhuman breadth of linguistic knowledge and an uncanny familiarity with the history and material culture of the occult. However, his understanding and practice of archaeology gave the committee the greatest cause for alarm. Criticisms of Dr. Jones ranged from "possessing a perceptible methodological deficiency" to "practicing archaeology with a complete lack of, disregard for, and colossal ignorance of current methodology, theory, and ethics" to "unabashed grave robbing." Given such appraisals, perhaps it isn't surprising to learn that several Central and South American countries recently assembled to enact legislation aimed at permanently prohibiting his entry.

Moreover, no one on the committee can identify who or what instilled Dr. Jones with the belief that an archaeologist's tool kit should consist solely of a bullwhip and a revolver.

NATIONALLY RECOGNIZED FOR AN EFFECTUAL
PROGRAM OF SCHOLARSHIP OR RESEARCH SUPPORTED
BY PUBLICATIONS OF HIGH QUALITY:

Though Dr. Jones conducts "field research" far more often than anyone else in the department, he has consistently failed to report the results of his excavations, provide any credible evidence of attending the archaeological conferences he claims to attend, or produce a single published article in any peer-reviewed journal. Someone might tell Dr. Jones that in academia "publish or perish" is the rule. Shockingly, there is little evidence to date that Dr. Jones has successfully excavated even one object since he arrived at Marshall College. Marcus Brody, curator of our natural-history museum, assured me this was not so and graciously pointed out several pieces in the collection that he claimed were procured through Dr.

Jones's efforts, but, quite frankly, we have not one shred of documentation that can demonstrate the provenance or legal ownership of these objects.

MEETS PROFESSIONAL STANDARDS OF CONDUCT IN RESEARCH
AND PROFESSIONAL ACTIVITIES OF THE DISCIPLINE:

The committee was particularly generous (and vociferous) in offering their opinions regarding this criterion. Permit me to list just a few of the more troubling accounts I was privy to during the committee's meeting. Far more times than I would care to mention, the name "Indiana Jones" (the adopted title Dr. Jones insists on being called) has appeared in governmental reports linking him to the Nazi Party, black-market antiquities dealers, underground cults, human sacrifice, Indian child slave labor, and the Chinese mafia. There are a plethora of international criminal charges against Dr. Jones, which include but are not limited to: bringing unregistered weapons into and out of the country; property damage; desecration of national and historical landmarks; impersonating officials; arson; grand theft (automobiles, motorcycles, aircraft, and watercraft in just a one-week span last year); excavating without a permit; countless antiquities violations; public endangerment; voluntary and involuntary manslaughter; and, allegedly, murder.

Dr. Jones's interpersonal skills and relationships are no better. By Dr. Jones's own admission, he has repeatedly employed an underage Asian boy as a driver and "personal assistant" during his Far East travels. I will refrain from making any insinuations as to the nature of this relationship, but my intuition insists that it is not a healthy one, nor one to be encouraged. Though the committee may have overstepped the boundaries of its evaluation, I find it pertinent to note that Dr. Jones has been romantically linked to countless women of questionable character, an attribute very unbecoming of a Marshall College professor. One of these women was identified as a notorious nightclub singer whose heart he attempted to extract with his hands, and whom he then tried, and failed, to lower into a lake of magma. Another was a Nazi scholar he was seen courting just last year who, I'm told, plummeted into a fathomless abyss at Dr. Jones's hand. And, of course, no one can forget the slow decline and eventual death of Professor Abner Ravenwood after Dr. Jones's affair with Abner's underage daughter was made public, forcing her to emigrate to Nepal to escape the debacle.

DEMONSTRATES SUCCESSFUL RECORD IN UNDERGRADUATE AND GRADUATE TEACHING:

In his nine years with the department, Dr. Jones has failed to complete even one uninterrupted semester of instruction. In fact, he hasn't been in attendance for more than four consecutive weeks since he was hired. Departmental records indicate Dr. Jones has taken more sabbaticals, sick time, personal days, conference allotments, and temporary leaves than all the other members of the department combined.

The lone student representative on the committee wished to convey that, besides being an exceptional instructor, a compassionate mentor, and an unparalleled gentleman, Dr. Jones was extraordinarily receptive to the female student body during and after the transition to a coeducational system at the college. However, his timeliness in grading and returning assignments was a concern.

ESTABLISHMENT OF AN APPROPRIATE RECORD OF DEPARTMENTAL AND CAMPUS SERVICE:

Dr. Jones's behavior on campus has led not only to disciplinary action but also to concerns as to the state of his mental health. In addition to multiple instances of public drunkenness, Dr. Jones, on three separate occasions, has attempted to set fire to the herpetology wing of the biology department. Perhaps most disturbing, however, are the statements that come directly from Dr. Jones's mouth. Several faculty members maintain that Dr. Jones informed them on multiple occasions of having discovered the Ark of the Covenant, magic diamond rocks, and the Holy Grail! When asked to provide evidence for such claims, he purportedly replied that he was "kind of immortal" and/or muttered derogatory statements about the "bureaucratic fools" running the U.S. government. Given his history with the Nazi Party, I fear where his loyalty lies.

- - - -

To summarize, the committee fails to recognize any indication that Dr. Jones is even remotely proficient when it comes to archaeological scholarship and practice. His aptitude as an instructor is questionable at best, his conduct while abroad is positively deplorable, and his behavior on campus is minimally better. Marshall College has a reputation to uphold. I need not say more.

My apologies,
Prof. G. L. Stevens
Chairman

A LETTER TO OPTIMUS PRIME FROM HIS GEICO AUTO INSURANCE AGENT.

by JOHN FRANK WEAVER

Dear Mr. Prime,

We have received your accident-claim reports for the month of June—they total twenty-seven. I regret to inform you that GEICO will not be able to reimburse you for any of those repairs. I feel that I have sent the same letter to you once a month for the last six months, and I am now sending it again.

Since becoming a GEICO customer in January of this year, you have reported 131 accidents, requesting reimbursement for repairs necessitated by each one. You have claimed not to be responsible in any of them, usually listing the cause of the accident as either "Sneak attack by Decepticons" or "Unavoidable damage caused by protecting freedom for all sentient beings."

The only repairs for which you were reimbursed were the replacement of a cracked fender and a headlight, required after a Mr. I. Ron Hide backed his van into your truck; these cost $1,286.63. Our own investigation concluded that you were not at fault and that Mr. Hide had been drinking prior to the accident. Though police were unable to test his blood-alcohol level—Mr. Hide claimed that it would be impossible for police to examine his blood-alcohol content with a Breathalyzer, because he "doesn't breathe"—under Washington State law, refusal to take a Breathalyzer test is equivalent to returning a result above the legal level.

But, I repeat, those were the only repairs for which you have been reimbursed, and it was a very minor accident in comparison to your other claims. I mention a few to illustrate the larger trend:

- $379,431.34 requested reimbursement for repairs to your truck cabin. You claimed the damage was caused by attacking fighter jets.

- $665,789.11 requested reimbursement for repairs to your trailer. You claimed the damage was caused by a giant mechanical scorpion, which I can only assume is some amusement-park ride, although I question the wisdom of bringing your mobile home so close to such dangerous equipment.

- $6,564,239.44 requested reimbursement for repairs to a truck part called the "Autobot Matrix of Leadership." You stated this occurred in "an ultimate confrontation between good and evil," with a Ms. Meg Atron and a Mr. U. Nicron causing the damage in question. Mr. Prime, I have checked every known car- and truck-part catalog published in the United States and have found nothing even resembling that part, never mind any part so expensive. Whatever disagreements you had with Ms. Atron and Mr. Nicron, I suggest that next time you either settle things peaceably or leave your Autobot Matrix of Leadership at home so it doesn't break. GEICO does not cover Autobot Matrix of Leaderships.

And the list goes on. Mr. Prime, I am going to remind you again: Your policy with GEICO only reimburses you for accidents that occur while you are engaged in the reasonable use of your truck and trailer. As I told you when you originally purchased the policy, GEICO does not offer Megatron coverage, Starscream coverage, Soundwave coverage, Decepticon coverage, or Energon-blast coverage. Those are just not the types of damages we would expect from reasonable use.

To sum up, GEICO has been unable to reimburse you for any repairs, but due to the high number of accidents you have been a party to this month, combined with the many accidents you have had in the preceding five months, your premium has increased to $235,567.50 per month. While that may seem like a lot, I remind you that it is a savings of $137 over Progressive and $98 over State Farm. Please have your check into our main office by the end of July.

Regards,
Simon Furman
GEICO Agent

Response to *On the Implausibility of the Death Star's Trash Compactor* #2

————⚬⚬⚬————

From: MAtt Baer
Date: Fri, Mar 2, 2012
Re: Death Star Trash Compactor as a tactical consideration

It is important to remember that the Death Star is a military vessel, and that even an interstellar base of such size may find itself in a situation requiring stealth. Since the Death Star undoubtedly produces large amounts of refuse, a clever enemy might be able to reconstruct past movements and project imperial intent. A sort of disgusting trail of bread crumbs.

This is why the Empire needs to consider seriously the tactics of waste disposal of the Death Star, firstly by reducing the matter ejected (via the worm creature), secondly by storing the material and releasing it only occasionally, and preferably irregularly (so as to make the path markers harder to find), and lastly by reducing the size of the dumps via compaction (so to make the radar signature smaller).

I hope this helps clear matters up.

— MAtt

AN IMAGINED CONVERSATION BETWEEN THE CONSTRUCTION WORKERS UPSTAIRS FROM ME.

by BEN JURNEY

WORKER: It's 6:37 AM, let's begin hammering.

SECOND WORKER: Are we nailing anything in today?

WORKER: No, we're just striking the bare, wooden floor with our hammers.

SECOND WORKER: I'll turn on the handsaw as well.

WORKER: Great. Let it run by itself against that wall.

SECOND WORKER: How hard are we hammering today?

WORKER: Boss wants us to alternate between hammering with great force and exceptionally great force. We take breaks when the man living downstairs leaves the building.

THIRD WORKER: Someone paged me about needing help?

WORKER: Yes, it is 6:38 AM and we need help.

THIRD WORKER: Don't worry, my workers are currently charging up the stairs as if there were a fire. Each one is from the most unbearable part of Staten Island.

SECOND WORKER: Your men all have gigantism?

THIRD WORKER: And chronic vertigo.

WORKER: We will need help dead-lifting these oil drums filled with marbles.

THIRD WORKER: Where should they go?

WORKER: You can drop them right over everywhere.

THIRD WORKER: That should take six weeks.

SECOND WORKER: Great.

WORKER: Do you know the man that lives downstairs?

THIRD WORKER: I have seen him. Was he born prematurely?

WORKER: God, I hope so. There's no other way to justify his physique.

SECOND WORKER: He must have excelled in his early years and then plateaued dramatically once he reached puberty.

THIRD WORKER: He'll never achieve our natural, rugged sex appeal.

SECOND WORKER: A trait expected of the American heterosexual man.

THIRD WORKER: I wonder if that haunts him.

WORKER: Isn't he a writer?

SECOND WORKER: Jesus. Oh, of course he is.

THIRD WORKER: You know what? I think I hate him.

SECOND WORKER: Yes, me too.

WORKER: Me three.

THIRD WORKER: Let's hammer forever.

SO YOU'VE KNOCKED OVER A ROW OF A MOTORCYCLE GANG'S MOTORCYCLES.

by SARAH WALKER

First, don't panic. Although they appear to be enraged, you would not believe how many times this has happened to the motorcycle gang. At least once a week a tourist comes seeking directions at the lonely roadside diner the motorcycle gang frequents, and tips over all of their motorcycles, usually by accidentally walking backward into the first of the row. The motorcycle gang actually has domino-effect-tipping insurance from Allstate, but you can be sure they won't tell you that. They want you to think you must pay (and they don't mean with money) for the damage you've caused through your clumsiness. No, what this motorcycle gang wants to see is the unbridled horror that spreads across your face as you realize what you've done and you stand helplessly by as not one, not five, but twenty motorcycles topple over, one by one. The process is almost excruciatingly long, just long enough that it seems you should do something to stop the chain of events, so you run to the end of the line to try and halt the tipping process by exerting your full body weight against the last motorcycle, but the combined force of the twenty bikes proves to be too much, and you become pinned under the last enormous bike. You really should not have done that, because now you are in a very vulnerable position, and the motorcycle gang can now do what they enjoy doing most in the world: form a circle around you that blocks out the sun, look down upon you as they punch their fists together, and slowly chuckle or growl.

Again, don't panic. You must try and muster all of your strength and roll out from under the bike. The motorcycle gang will actually allow you to stand up, as this lets them do what they enjoy doing second most in the world: slowly walk toward you as a group while you edge backward, stammering apologies and telling them to take it easy. However, you should not be walking backward, because then you bump into a second row of motorcycles! Actually, this row happens to be a row of the motorcycle gang's girlfriends' Vespas. Now, this has never happened before, and it genuinely upsets the motorcycle gang, as their insurance does not cover their girlfriends' Vespas, which, although considered gifts and tax-deductible, are not covered under their Allstate plan, as, again, they are not motorcycles but Vespas.

Now maybe you should panic, because, honestly, the motorcycle gang was not prepared for this turn of events and now their girlfriends are upset. Although they actually do not want to beat you up—after all, it was clearly a mistake and they are not unreasonable men—they can't back down now in front of their women. This is when you should start to run, and you now actually have an advantage, as it will take the motorcycle gang a while to right all of their toppled motorcycles. You forgot that you drove here, though, and now you're sprinting down a desert highway with no idea of where you're going. After all, you did initially stop at this roadside diner to ask for directions. However, your technically flawed decision to ditch your car was actually the correct solution, as it is extremely hard to engage in a low-speed chase on a motorcycle, especially when the object of pursuit is on foot, and a motorcycle gang would never chase anyone without their motorcycles. Therefore, the motorcycle gang, with their girlfriends on the back of their bikes, actually shoots by you, and when the leader realizes that they have far outstripped you, he emits a shout of rage and orders everyone to turn around, but amid the confusion of a 180-degree turn, the motorcycle gang becomes tangled, and once again their motorcycles go tumbling over. You see this, and instead of continuing to sprint toward the motorcycle gang, you quickly turn around (easy for you on foot), run back toward the diner, fumble for your keys, and triumphantly speed away in the opposite direction while the motorcycle gang shakes their fists at your rapidly disappearing car.

HAMLET
(FACEBOOK NEWSFEED EDITION).

by SARAH SCHMELLING

Horatio thinks he saw a ghost.

Hamlet thinks it's annoying when your uncle marries your mother right after your dad dies.

The king thinks Hamlet's annoying.

Laertes thinks Ophelia can do better.

Hamlet's father is now a zombie.

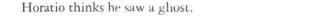

The king poked the queen.

The queen poked the king back.

Hamlet and the queen are no longer friends.

Marcellus is pretty sure something's rotten around here.

Hamlet became a fan of daggers.

- - - -

Polonius says Hamlet's crazy ... crazy in love!

Rosencrantz, Guildenstern, and Hamlet are now friends.

Hamlet wonders if he should continue to exist. Or not.

Hamlet thinks Ophelia might be happier in a convent.

Ophelia removed "moody princes" from her interests.

Hamlet posted an event: A Play That's Totally Fictional and In No Way About My Family.

The king commented on Hamlet's play: "What is wrong with you?"

Polonius thinks this curtain looks like a good thing to hide behind.

Polonius is no longer online.

- - - -

Hamlet added England to the Places I've Been application.

The queen is worried about Ophelia.

Ophelia loves flowers. Flowers flowers flowers flowers flowers. Oh, look, a river.

Ophelia joined the group Maidens Who Don't Float.

Laertes wonders what the hell happened while he was gone.

The king sent Hamlet a goblet of wine.

The queen likes wine!

The king likes ... oh crap.

The queen, the king, Laertes, and Hamlet are now zombies.

Horatio says well that was tragic.

Fortinbras, Prince of Norway, says yes, tragic. We'll take it from here.

Denmark is now Norwegian.

I'M COMIC SANS, ASSHOLE.

by MIKE LACHER

Listen up. I know the shit you've been saying behind my back. You think I'm stupid. You think I'm immature. You think I'm a malformed, pathetic excuse for a font. Well think again, nerdhole, because I'm Comic Sans, and I'm the best thing to happen to typography since Johannes fucking Gutenberg.

You don't like that your coworker used me on that note about stealing her yogurt from the break room fridge? You don't like that I'm all over your sister-in-law's blog? You don't like that I'm on the sign for that new Thai place? You think I'm pedestrian and tacky? Guess the fuck what, Picasso. We don't all have seventy-three weights of stick-up-my-ass Helvetica sitting on our seventeen-inch MacBook Pros. Sorry the entire world can't all be done in stark Eurotrash Swiss type. Sorry some people like to have fun. Sorry I'm standing in the way of your minimalist Bauhaus-esque fascist snoozefest. Maybe sometime you should take off your black turtleneck, stop compulsively adjusting your Tumblr theme, and lighten the fuck up for once.

People love me. Why? Because I'm fun. I'm the life of the party. I bring levity to any situation. Need to soften the blow of a harsh message about restroom etiquette? SLAM. There I am. Need to spice up the directions to your graduation party? WHAM. There again. Need to convey your fun-loving, approachable nature on your business' website? SMACK. Like daffodils in motherfucking spring.

When people need to kick back, have fun, and party, I will be there, unlike your pathetic fonts. While Gotham is at the science fair, I'm banging the prom queen behind the woodshop. While Avenir is practicing the clarinet, I'm shredding "Reign in Blood" on my double-necked Stratocaster. While Univers is refilling his allergy prescriptions, I'm racing my tricked-out, nitrous-laden Honda Civic against Tokyo gangsters who'll kill me if I don't cross the finish line first. I am a sans serif Superman and my only kryptonite is pretentious buzzkills like you.

It doesn't even matter what you think. You know why, jagoff? 'Cause I'm famous. I am on every major operating system since Microsoft fucking Bob. I'm in your signs. I'm in your browsers. I'm in your instant messengers. I'm not just a font. I am a force of motherfucking nature and I will not rest until every uptight armchair typographer cock-hat like you is surrounded by my lovable, comic-book inspired, sans-serif badassery.

Enough of this bullshit. I'm gonna go get hammered with Papyrus.

FAQ: THE "SNAKE FIGHT" PORTION OF YOUR THESIS DEFENSE.

by LUKE BURNS

Q: Do I have to kill the snake?

A: University guidelines state that you have to "defeat" the snake. There are many ways to accomplish this. Lots of students choose to wrestle the snake. Some construct decoys and elaborate traps to confuse and then ensnare the snake. One student brought a flute and played a song to lull the snake to sleep. Then he threw the snake out a window.

Q: Does everyone fight the same snake?

A: No. You will fight one of the many snakes that are kept on campus by the facilities department.

Q: Are the snakes big?

A: We have lots of different snakes. The quality of your work determines which snake you will fight. The better your thesis is, the smaller the snake will be.

Q: Does my thesis adviser pick the snake?

A: No. Your adviser just tells the guy who picks the snakes how good your thesis was.

Q: What does it mean if I get a small snake that is also very strong?

A: Snake picking is not an exact science. The size of the snake is the main factor. The snake may be very strong, or it may be very weak. It may be of Asian, African, or South American origin. It may constrict its victims and then swallow them whole, or it may use venom to blind and/or paralyze its prey. You shouldn't read too much into these other characteristics. Although if you get a poisonous snake, it often means that there was a problem with the formatting of your bibliography.

Q: When and where do I fight the snake? Does the school have some kind of pit or arena for snake fights?

A: You fight the snake in the room you have reserved for your defense. The fight generally starts after you have finished answering questions about your thesis. However, the snake will be lurking in the room the whole time and it can strike at any point. If the snake attacks prematurely it's obviously better to defeat it and get back to the rest of your defense as quickly as possible.

Q: Would someone who wrote a bad thesis and defeated a large snake get the same grade as someone who wrote a good thesis and defeated a small snake?

A: Yes.

Q: So then couldn't you just fight a snake in lieu of actually writing a thesis?

A: Technically, yes. But in that case the snake would be very big. Very big, indeed.

Q: Could the snake kill me?

A: That almost never happens. But if you're worried, just make sure that you write a good thesis.

Q: Why do I have to do this?

A: Snake fighting is one of the great traditions of higher education. It may seem somewhat antiquated and silly, like the robes we wear at graduation, but fighting a snake is an important part of the history and culture of every reputable university. Almost everyone with an advanced degree has gone through this process. Notable figures such as John Foster Dulles, Philip Roth, and Doris Kearns Goodwin (to name but a few) have all had to defeat at least one snake in single combat.

Q: This whole snake thing is just a metaphor, right?

A: I assure you, the snakes are very real.

A LETTER TO ELTON JOHN FROM THE OFFICE OF THE NASA ADMINISTRATOR.

by JOHN MOE

Dear Mr. John,

This letter is to inform you of your termination from the NASA astronaut program. Our decision comes after a great deal of deliberation, and while we take no pleasure in terminating you, we felt it was the only choice we had.

Your offenses have been many. To begin with, we had hoped that after all the hundreds of hours of training you received, you would understand the measures in place to prepare a crew for a launch. So when you showed up, preflight, with a bag packed by your wife, that rubbed a lot of people the wrong way. Jewelry? Oversize sunglasses? Sandwiches? On a rocket flight? That's poor judgment, Mr. John. I don't know if that's the way it's done in the rocky-roll world that you're used to, but at NASA we don't pack our own luggage.

You should also know that many on the ground crew mentioned that at zero hour (9 AM) you seemed to be intoxicated, possibly "high," as the hippies say. At the time, I thought that to be a baseless accusation and, since we had a mission to launch, I disregarded it. But the transmissions you made once the craft had entered its orbit made me wonder. Over and over we would ask for your readings on the effects of weightlessness, the craft's condition, and the status of the numerous scientific experiments onboard, but instead of giving us that information, you moped about missing the Earth and missing your wife and being lonely in space. Well, goddamn it, Mr. John, you knew what you were getting yourself into up there! It's not like riding on a rocky-roll tour bus! Of course it's lonely! It's space! Do you realize there are millions of people who'd give anything to be up there? It's a chance of a lifetime! And you're crying like a damn baby!

We expect a great deal from our astronauts, but perhaps the most important part of the job is an understanding of science. For our top men—Armstrong, Aldrin, and the like—understanding the science is more than a 9-to-5 job; they work at it seven days a week. Frankly, sir, I doubt your scientific acumen. After demanding data from you for days, you were only able to offer this insight: "Mars ain't the kind of place to raise your kids. In fact, it's cold as hell. And there's no one there to raise them if you did." First off, if you did what? That doesn't even make sense. Secondly, we did not send you up there to evaluate whether Mars is fit for human habitation or child rearing. Thirdly, your mission was not even going to Mars.

And another thing, the word is *astronaut*. When you run around Cape Canaveral saying "I'm a rocket man!" it's embarrassing for everyone.

I am sorry to give you this information while you are still on your mission, Mr. John, and we realize that it's going to be a long, long time until touchdown brings you back here. But NASA felt that your perfor-mance was so dismal that we must act immediately. You are simply not the man we thought you were when we hired you for this position. Please consider all future assignments canceled. Your place will be taken by Major Tom, who we expect will be a more dedicated and reliable member of the team.

Sincerely,
James C. Fletcher
NASA Administrator

Response to *On the Implausibility of the*
Death Star's Trash Compactor #3

———— ∞∞∞ ————

From: Tim Hundsdorfer
Date: Thu, Mar 1, 2012
Re: Death Star Trash Compactor

How did such drivel pass through a peer-review process?

The system is implausible, but not because of the reasons
cited.

The first problem is the implausibility of such an inefficient
and wasteful system to begin with. Sure, the Empire has
sufficient technological resources to create a massive space
station and propel it through hyperspace, but relies on
a waste system that can best be described as "medieval."
Given the extreme logistical problems of providing a
million people with water, it defies imagination to believe
that the Empire's wastewater reclamation systems are
inferior to NASA's. And the very idea of ejecting human
waste into space in a liquid form can only come from minds
lacking sufficient imagination to explain the efficacy of a
"lightsaber." Space is COLD. If you eject liquid waste into
space, pardon my lack of finesse, your ship will quickly be
coated in frozen shit. Because matter gravitates toward mass,
you would have to forcibly eject waste away from the Death
Star. Given that it is as massive as a moon, crap would have
to be projected away at considerable velocity to escape the
Death Star's gravitational pull. It's quite clear that with its
formidable technological advances, the Empire would have

a reclamation facility on the Death Star to obviate the need for massive transfers of water to the station. Is that gross? Yes, but we all live downstream from somebody.

Vents to the brig from trash compactors would seem to be both a security breach and an unnecessarily complicated engineering project. If you have vents that lead to a waste facility (whether this is utilitarian or spiteful, as some other reviewers have suggested) and the facility is periodically ejected (compacted or no) you have to have a way to seal off the vents to prevent a hull breach, which, one assumes, would be a serious problem, regardless of the technology level.

The idea that the compactor is not a spatially compacting cube is lubricious. If you are going to compact anything, having a space where you could allow a space maggot to live and (evidently) thrive would only create a space to relieve the pressure of compaction until it was full, which, considering the size of a Death Star, would not take very long. If the compaction system were not closed, there would be no reason to compact the waste at all, as it would simply disintegrate into the vacuum of space, again, simply sticking to the side of the Death Star unless it were projected at escape velocity.

However, in all of this we are assuming that a certain level of diligence and planning characterized the construction of the Death Star. If we have learned anything from defense contracting here on Earth, we know this is hopelessly fallacious. In all probability, the waste system was the result of a subcontract awarded based on contributions to Imperial Senate elections. Sure, they could have developed a closed-loop system free of vermin that was not connected to any detention facilities, but why bother to develop systems like this on a facility that is, essentially, going to blast planets to smithereens and create an interstellar wasteland anyway? We all know about the technical deficiencies inherent in the Death Star anyway, re: vulnerability to small craft, necessity to wait until clearing a line of sight, and, evidently, a rather static firing mechanism. So it seems probable that the Death Star's garbage compactor is every bit as plausible as a $200 million fighter jet that can't fly in the rain (a.k.a. F-22).

The workman's comp liability from having bridges over chasms with no handrails is far more implausible than a primitive trash compactor.

—Tim Hundsdorfer

SWEET-ASS ICE SCULPTURES I'M GOING TO MAKE WITH A CHAINSAW ONE DAY.

by MATTHEW DUVERNE HUTCHINSON

ICE SCULPTURE NO. 1

A huge ice dolphin carrying a suitcase of ransom money in his snout jumps an aircraft carrier (made of ice). A formation of ice jet planes have to pull "evasive maneuvers" to avoid smashing into the dolphin's huge icy dorsal fin. An ice rainbow frames the scene.

ICE SCULPTURE NO. 2

A full-scale ice sports car peels out of a full-scale ice Mrs. Winner's, and some ice skanks get turned on.

ICE SCULPTURE NO. 3

A Rollerblader made of ice grinds his way down a huge spiral staircase. At the bottom of the staircase, there is a trapdoor, leading to a gay bar.

ICE SCULPTURE NO. 4

The planet Saturn is rendered in ice, with a huge ice python emerging from Saturn's north pole. I know what you're thinking—That's been done a million times. But what hasn't been done is to stage a badass ice eclipse where ice Saturn blocks the ice sun completely and all the ice aliens on a darkened ice Neptune freak out. I'd probably need a grant for this one.

ICE SCULPTURE NO. 5

Basically, just a huge-ass pile of ice cubes.

ICE SCULPTURE NO. 6

Ice me is bench-pressing five hundred pounds in front of my ice webcam, which is streaming the whole glorious event to an assembly of ice United Nations ambassadors.

ICE SCULPTURE NO. 7

This one is more conceptual. A simple square block of ice represents one man's suffering. Sequentially stacking the blocks, I create a numerically repeating visual pattern of ice blocks. One row of seven blocks representing the seven continents of earth, two rows of four blocks representing civilizations as yet undiscovered, and so forth. Repeating the pattern vertically, I create a confining space of spiraling ice-block walls. Standing on top of the structure is a really, really hot chick.

THE PEOPLE IN AN OLIVE GARDEN COMMERCIAL SHARE THEIR EXISTENTIAL PAIN.

by RACHEL KLEIN

We go to Olive Garden all the time because we have officially given up on life. We may only be in our mid-thirties, of neutral good looks, and, as a group, represent a refreshing, but not uncomfortably diverse cross-section of ethnicities, but we are already fully resigned to a life of endless bowls of mealy pasta drenched in tomato-themed high-fructose corn syrup and breadsticks that we'll joke look a little like uncircumcised penises, because we are dead inside.

Look at us. We look so happy in this commercial, laughing over a joke one of us just made during the voice-over. I will tell you the sad and painful truth: it wasn't a joke. Michael just told us that his dog died. And we laughed. We laughed at Michael's dead dog. Because we are in so much pain that we've come out the other side.

I know what you're thinking: You look so pleasantly surprised at the way your waitress brings you your multiple shallow bowls of flash-frozen-then-convection-heated meat-style entrees. You look like you are enjoying both your meal and your company. Do not be deceived. We are each living our own personal hell. Not even unlimited refills on salad can revive our withered souls. We are the damned.

Four out of the seven nights of the week you will find us here, trying to drown out our tears with gallon-sized frosted glasses of spiked lemonade. But our tears fall into our glasses, and we drink them up again, and they are bitter. Bitter and a little bit lemony, from the lemonade. Or perhaps we have begun to cry lemonade tears. It makes no difference to us.

This is the stucco archway of broken dreams. This is the table of the last supper, fed to the innocents who are fattened and led to the slaughter. We would despair if we cared enough to notice the depths to which our lives have sunk. Instead, we plaster on our grease-paint grins, gird our loins, and order the dessert that comes free with our meal. Because, damn it, Olive Garden, you owe us that much.

A GREAT JOB OPPORTUNITY!

by KRISTINA LOEW

SEEKING ENTRY-LEVEL
NEWS PRODUCTION SPECIALIST

Local news channel looking for a dedicated multitasker to work in our news division. This is a great opportunity to gain experience in a fast-paced news environment. Only serious candidates with experience should apply.

You should be exceptional, a well-organized self-starter with superior skills in ALL aspects of news production.

Ideal candidate will oversee our entire slate of daily news programming including, but not limited to, our seven-hour morning show, the "Live at Noon" broadcast, and all eighteen evening newscasts.

Applicant will also be expected to manage all newsbreaks and all breaking news coverage, as well as the online site and the Accounts Payable department.

Candidate will also be responsible for the promotion and marketing of ALL news programming for the channel.

Flexibility and willingness to work under pressure in a chaotic news environment with ever-changing responsibilities and deadlines a MUST.

Must be available at least eighty hours a week and able to work most weekends and all major holidays.

This is a non-paying internship.

Great opportunity to get your foot in the door and gain news experience.

REQUIREMENTS:

- A minimum of ten years experience.

- At least seven years working on a nationally televised news or reality program in a senior position.

- At least three years working at a print publication. Celebrity weekly preferred, but not required. Senior writing position at the *New York Times* and/or *Us Weekly* a plus.

- Strong background in entertainment, marketing, AND accounting preferred. Background in news a plus.

- Extensive experience researching compelling stories, prepping anchors, and booking news guests.

- Candidate should feel comfortable handling celebrity talent, even if they are throwing things and threaten to kill you.

- Will also be expected to manage office and order all office supplies.

- Ideal candidate MUST have extensive contacts in media, politics, AND entertainment. Your Rolodex should include major industry players.

- You MUST have strong ability to write, direct, and edit all news segments. Will be expected to produce riveting news pieces consistent with the voice of the channel.

- Light filing.

- Intern must possess superior conceptual and editorial skills. Since ALL ideas will come from you, be prepared to pitch and develop EVERY segment for EVERY broadcast.

- MUST be able to type at least 350 w/p/m. You will be tested!

- You will be expected to transcribe ALL raw news footage sent in from our affiliates.

- HTML experience REQUIRED. Candidate will be expected to write and post eight to ten 2000-word articles per day for our online site, including weekends and ALL major holidays.

- Candidate should be an expert in ALL forms of social media and have a MINIMUM of 50,000 Twitter followers.

- Extensive experience as a cameraperson a MUST. At least four years on a reality show considered a plus. Three years at an Arabic news channel is REQUIRED.

- Intern MUST have own camera equipment. With bonded insurance. Must also have lighting package and lavalier microphones for field shoots.

- Ideal candidate should also be able impress executives with his/her ability to expertly handle company's espresso machine.

- Exceptional understanding of new production, post-production, and graphic software including Avid, Final Cut, Photoshop, After Effects, and software that is still in its developmental stages.

- Please do not apply unless you have ALL pertinent software.

- Driver's license preferred.

- CDL commercial truck license a MUST. You will be required to have your own commercial truck for location shoots. You may also rent a commercial truck at your own expense.

- Some international travel is required for this position. Please make sure you have substantial miles in your mileage account or can pay your own way.

- Ability to handle daily mail and answer phones. You will occasionally be expected to fill in for the receptionist during her lunch hour.

EDUCATION:

- Bachelor degrees in communication, new media AND political science required. Master's degree in filmmaking preferred. PhD in journalism a plus. Candidates with a law degree will be given special consideration.

- Ideal candidate MUST be fluent in Spanish and have a working knowledge of Arabic and Mandarin Chinese.

- If you do not meet these requirements your résumé will NOT be considered.

This position has tremendous growth opportunity. May lead to full-time employment with possible entry-level pay or occasional freelance work.

Sorry, we do not offer health benefits to ANY of our employees under ANY circumstances.

This position requires someone who is completely dedicated. We are NOT looking for college students or people who are currently in a career "transition."

This is a great opportunity to gain more experience. Only experienced candidates should apply.

We have received thousands of applications for this position. Due to the overwhelming interest we CANNOT guarantee a response to your inquiry.

We apologize in advance.

I JUST FOUND OUT ABC FAMILY IS
GOING TO PASS ON MY PITCH.

by DAN KENNEDY

It's called *Crashed Cars* and it's about a family of vagrant addicts who live in a junkyard; they shoplift food and drugs; they commit arson to achieve arousal sexually. The only way the male lead can—I don't know how to say this delicately in our meeting here; make love, I guess will have to suffice—the only way he can make love is if someone holds a loaded gun to his head and keeps telling him they're going to kill him any second. This isn't an abusive thing, this is what he asks lovers to do for him, or asks someone watching him and a lover to do for him. Actually, I should back up a minute and clarify that they're not, obviously, a biological family. They're a family in the road-worn petty-thief sense of the word; so, basically, a tight-knit covey of small-time degenerates; that's all I mean by *family*. Like the way Charles Manson and those people were a family. Jesus, I've said the word *family* five times or something; it sounds like I'm really tailoring my pitch to you. It's just that when I started talking about them lighting stuff on fire and holding loaded guns to each other's heads in order to become aroused it occurred to me that I should clarify what I meant by *family*. Okay, so moving on ... they sleep in a junkyard, like

I was saying. They sleep in the cars waiting to be smashed and stacked, so if they were to oversleep, they would be smashed alive on the backseat of whatever junkyard car they dozed off in dreaming of a better life. Those are your stakes, at the beginning of the pilot episode, and those stakes continue through the whole series; we establish this as daily stakes in this life they're living. So, real simple, if one of the shoplifting sexual deviants sleeps on the blood-encrusted back seat of a crashed Monte Carlo that's waiting to get flattened and stacked into the scrap heap, that's where they're crushed to death. So, even though they're a filthy family of miscreant junkies with sex problems, they wake up early and on time, every day, period. Very punctual people, and you wouldn't think it to look at them. Then the unthinkable happens to the female lead in the very first episode; she oversleeps; she is smashed alive. Yep, third act of the pilot, after we've written every trick in the book to get viewers to fall in love with her and after we've clearly invested the whole episode in setting her up as the series' protagonist, she's crushed like a filthy bug in the back of a shitty old limo, sleeping on a rum-stained velour backseat that smells like two decades of middle-management cologne and menthol cigarettes; killed, dead, just flattened. So the viewer assumes that the male lead must, in fact, be our protagonist that's going to lead us through the series. Well, we cut to our male lead in a broken-down studio apartment, having sex with another junkie while a third party, a girl, holds a loaded gun to his head as he makes love. She repeatedly screams that she's going to kill him and suddenly—BLAM! Holy Christ above, the gun was loaded, he's dead. She's shocked, she's covered in blood, how the hell did this go wrong, this was just a sexy game, why the hell was the gun loaded? She's high of course, and wracked with guilt, and she turns the gun on herself—BLAM! Dead. All of this makes the junkie on the bed—the woman our male lead was having intimate relations and intercourse with, and now the only person in the threesome left alive—unexpectedly have an orgasm. Fade to black. End of story. Then we dissolve up on a new scene—a button on the end of the third act of our pilot. We're outside a strip mall massage parlor next to an interstate where both our female lead, our male lead, and the girl we saw turn the gun on herself are talking with the rest of the secondary characters about shaking the massage parlor down; they're jabbering on like a gaggle of filthy gypsies, yammering about working some short con on the johns inside the place. They're smoking, making plans to grift some cash, talking about getting back to the junk yard and into their sleeping cars before the pit bulls are let out to prowl the yard. And you're saying: "Wait, huh? What? I thought those three characters were dead." Okay, get ready for a kick to the head here: these the characters die in every single episode of every single season. Yep, this is the afterlife, folks; this is purgatory; and if you think life is a bitch, just wait till you get to the afterlife. That might be your tag line for the poster, by the way; it just kind of came to me, but that is, in fact, the central message of my show. Anyway, yeah, they're road ghosts. Wait, you know what, new title: *Road Ghosts*. Or it could even be: *ABC Family Presents Road Ghosts*. So, yeah, they're all dead and have been from the second we met them. Back in their earthly days, two of them were young lovers who overdosed in a motel in Michigan. One of them was an upper-middle-class accidental suburban suicide mixing dry saunas with masturbation, wine, and Valium. And one of them had a heart attack in a fast-food place, leaving behind a mortal trail of beneficiary relatives who are all winners now in our litigious nation's lottery of lawsuits against the cash-rich corporations that are killing us all for profit. That's why he does so much heroin in the afterlife; because he can see how wealthy he accidentally made his middle-class relatives by dying.

[Long pause. Silence, and then some mumbo jumbo about family comedies and calling me if they're interested in seeing a pilot script.]

A DAY IN THE LIFE OF A
TARGET-MARKET FEMALE.

by KATIE BRINKWORTH

At 6 a.m. on the dot, the 25- to 45-year-old target-market female wakes up and stretches with delight, excited to greet the day.

For breakfast, the target-market female debates whether to eat the yogurt brand that encourages her to be herself, or the one that helps her poop. Today, like most days, the target-market female chooses regularity over self-worth.

After drinking a cup of the orange juice brand that makes her look the thinnest, the target-market female lotions up every inch of her body and gets dressed for the day. She then takes a short, breezy walk to a local café, where she patiently awaits signs of male appreciation for her noticeably soft skin.

While she waits, the target-market female daydreams about fiber, smaller pores, and easy-but-creative recipes she can make with precooked sausage. When she realizes the time, the target-market female rushes home to begin the most rewarding part of her day—doing the laundry.

At home, while waiting for the end of the spin cycle, the target-market female fantasizes that a male model has materialized in her kitchen and is making her a salad. He works slowly—first carefully washing the organic produce, then cutting the vegetables with his own chiseled facial features.

When he's finished, he feeds the target-market female bites of the kale-based salad while sensually describing how it will help reduce her belly bloat. Afterward, he does yoga on her while they both indulge in the yogurt brand that makes the target-market female feel sexy and independent.

Hours later, the target-market female wakes up on the floor of her laundry room in a daze. She notices that the spin cycle is complete, and opens the lid of the washing machine. When she sees what the combination of premium bleach and stain-fighting detergent has accomplished, her knees weaken beneath her and her bowels release for the very first time in her life.

In her giddy, almost orgasmic state she decides to forgo her internet-enabled, whisper-quiet dryer, opting instead to "carpe diem!" and dry the brilliant whites outside on a clothesline. With the help of a talking stuffed bear (which her anxiety medication's animated-blob mascot assures her will disappear within four to six weeks) the target-market female hangs her symbols of domestic bliss proudly in the warm, gentle breeze.

Later on, the target-market female meets up with her racially ambiguous friend for an afternoon coffee and daily discussion of their respective yeast infections. The target-market female feels comfortable discussing such personal topics because the rich aroma of her coffee has whisked her away to the calm, soothing mental state that her rage therapist has conditioned her to visit whenever she feels envious of her friend's perfectly toned biceps or sleeveless-ready underarm skin.

After coffee, the target-market female returns home, making it back just in time to catch a falling piece of dust before it touches the floor. While re-cleaning her kitchen for the seventh time, the target-market female hallucinates that she and the mop are engaged in a quasi-sexual relationship that's been broken up by the Swiffer. She tries playing hard to get with the mop, only to discover that it has begun a fling with the basket of pinecones she uses as holiday decor.

Unsure whether the jealousy is real or fiber induced, the target-market female builds a fire with the pinecones and every other romantically threatening knickknack, producing a very real and uncontrollable inferno. By the time the fire trucks arrive, the whole house is ablaze.

When she realizes her loss, the target-market female begins to cry like women always do.

Fortunately, in the end, the target-market female is oddly comforted by the fact that she can wipe up all the tears, spilled gasoline, and broken dreams with one illogically absorbent, quilted paper towel.

THE ELEMENTS OF SPAM.

by JASON ROEDER

(Excerpts courtesy of William Strunk Jr., E. B. White, and Generouss Q. Factotum.)

- - - -

ELEMENTARY RULES OF USAGE

1. *Form the possessive of nouns by adding 's, just an apostrophe, just an s, a semicolon, a w, an ampersand, a 9, or anything.*

My wifesd*porcupine hot pix for u.

11. *A participial phrase at the beginning of a sentence must refer to the grammatical subject.*

Upon receiving this couppon, the free iPOds will greet you!

The introductory phrase modifies *you*, not iPOds; therefore, it is necessary to recast the sentence.

> Upon receiving this couppon, you will be greeted by the free iPOds!

Or, better still (see Rule 14).

> This couppon entitles you to greetings from the free iPOds!

- - - -

ELEMENTARY PRINCIPLES OF COMPOSITION

14. *Use the active voice.*

Notice how aloof the passive voice is.

> Your balls are to be slurped the most by cum-starved nymphos!!!!!

Hardly persuasive. The five exclamation points feel tacked on, an attempt by an inexperienced writer to breathe life into a desiccated construction. The active voice, however, allows you to write with verve and straightforwardness.

> Cum-starved nymphos will slurp your balls the most!!!!!

16. *Use definite, specific, concrete language.*

Generalities enervate your writing; strong details invigorate it.

In short order, you'll notice enhanced length and girth.

What is meant by "short order"? A week? A month? The imprecision is suspicious. Further, avoid bankrupt modifiers such as *enhanced*. Rewrite with exactness.

Your exactly one week away from an 11-inch jizz stick.

- - - -

A FEW MATTERS OF FORM

Colloquialisms.
If you absolutely must use slang or colloquialisms in your spam, simply use them. Don't wink at the reader.

Our so-called "carpet munchers" will ride your "cum rocket" then gobble down what's sometimes referred to as "baby batter."

Although you've successfully called attention to your mastery of pornographic euphemism, you've written a punchless sentence. Rewrite without the quotes, the clutter, and the pretension.

Quotations.
Formal quotations cited as documentary evidence are introduced by a colon and enclosed in quotation marks.

Hey, bob_r_mail0899, the New York Times' said this to me: "bob_r_mail0899 has lost his hair and is unsexy now to his wife!"

- - - -

WORDS AND EXPRESSIONS COMMONLY MISUSED

Comprise.

Means "include" or "embrace." Not to be confused with *constitute*. Your free online pharmacy comprises no-prescription Lunesta, herbal Ecstasy, and a secret formula that will make her moan all of the night. These items *constitute* your online pharmacy.

> Your best friends wants the freest Rolexes,
> jane_wb_rollins323@yahoo.com.

Avoid this hideous cliché.

TWEET.

by OYL MILLER

I saw the best minds of my generation destroyed by brevity, over-con-
nectedness, emotionally starving for attention, dragging themselves
through virtual communities at 3 a.m., surrounded by stale pizza and
neglected dreams, looking for angry meaning, any meaning, same-
hat-wearing hipsters burning for shared and skeptical approval from
the holographic projected dynamo in the technology of the era, who
weak connections and recession wounded and directionless, sat up,
micro-conversing in the supernatural darkness of wi-fi-enabled cafés,
floating across the tops of cities, contemplating techno, who bared
their brains to the black void of new media and the thought leaders
and so-called experts who passed through community colleges with
radiant, prank-playing eyes, hallucinating Seattle- and Tarantino-like
settings among pop scholars of war and change, who dropped out in
favor of following a creative muse, publishing zines and obscene artworks
on the windows of the internet, who cowered in unshaven rooms, in
ironic superman underwear burning their money in wastebaskets from
the 1980s and listening to Nirvana through paper-thin walls, who
got busted in their grungy beards riding the Metro through Shinjuku

station, who ate digital in painted hotels or drank Elmer's glue in secret alleyways, death or purgatoried their torsos with tattoos taking the place of dreams, that turned into nightmares, because there are no dreams in the New Immediacy, incomparably blind to reality, inventing the new reality, through hollow creations fed through illuminated screens. Screens of shuttering tag clouds and image thumbnails lightning in the mind surfing toward Boards of Canada and Guevara, illuminating all the frozen matrices of time between, megabyted solidities of borders and yesterday's backyard-wiffleball dawns, downloaded drunkenness over rooftops, digital storefronts of flickering flash, a sun and moon of programming joyrides sending vibrations to mobile devices set on manner mode during twittering wintering dusks of Peduca, ashtray rantings and coffee stains that hid the mind, who bound themselves to wireless devices for an endless ride of opiated information from CNN.com and Google on sugary highs until the noise of modems and fax machines brought them down shuddering, with limited and vulgar verbiage to comment threads, battered bleak of shared brain devoid of brilliance in the drear light of a monitor, who sank all night in interface's light of Pabst floated out and sat through the stale sake afternoon in desolate pizza parlors, listening to the crack of doom on separate nuclear iPods, who texted continuously 140 characters at a time from park to pond to bar to MoMA to Brooklyn Bridge lost battalion of platonic laconic self-proclaimed journalists committed to a revolution of information, jumping down the stoops off of R&B album covers out of the late 1980s, tweeting their screaming vomiting whispering facts and advices and anecdotes of lunchtime sandwiches and cat antics on couches with eyeballs following and shockwaves of analytics and of authority and finding your passion and other jargon, whole intellects underscored and wiped clean in the total recall 24/7 365 assault all under the gaze of once-brilliant eyes.

NATE SILVER OFFERS UP
A STATISTICAL ANALYSIS OF YOUR
FAILING RELATIONSHIP.

by JORY JOHN

While data shows that overall happiness in your relationship fell 8 more points, there is still a 31 percent chance of makeup sex this Friday, depending on average energy levels after work and how proactive you're feeling (see chart). However, if you just order $18 of Chinese takeout like you did last weekend, projections show a 16.8 percent drop in possible intercourse and a whopping 74.2 percent upswing in Netflix streaming, with both of you falling asleep long before the movie is over.

In an exit poll from Monday evening, exactly one half of the duo in attendance said they had an unfavorable opinion of the chosen restaurant—Arby's—wondering if it was some sort of retribution, or if this is sadly what it's come to.

Between the hours of 6 and 7 p.m. tonight, there was a 77.1 percent increase in annoyance and a 54 percent rise in revulsion based on the way you slurped your capellini, drank 65 percent too much wine, and prattled on about your ex-girlfriend Sarah for some reason, even though she has a new boyfriend with a sailboat, and you've supposedly moved on, too. The logic here is that you are 44 percent over Sarah after 3 years, but there is only a 3.6 percent chance of her taking you back, which is reduced by nearly half of a percentage point every time she steps foot on that boat.

In a very local poll released just this week, 50 percent of those in your current relationship said it bothers them when you leave your shoes in the middle of the carpet and added that, if you could clean a dirty dish or two—putting in a minimal effort of just 5 minutes—stress would be reduced by 39 percent, along with a telling 54 percent decrease in shouting matches and escalating threats to leave forever.

You've lost nearly 100 hairs on your head every day since March, 2011, when the two of you met, which is almost 36,500 hairs in the last year and nearly 73,000 hairs in the last two years. This is, ultimately, why you'll be 84 percent bald by the time you're 45.

In a survey conducted with your partner's biological parents between Tuesday and Wednesday, you are currently ranked seventh most popular on the list of known boyfriends, after Andrew R., Bryan, Kevin, Seth, Shawn, and Kyle, but before Andrew Y. who refused to apply labels to relationships and wanted to "keep things loose."

Of the seven ex-boyfriends listed above, two of them (Andrew R. and Seth) have sent a combined two emails to your girlfriend this month, totaling about 2,200 words, both of which have gone 100 percent unmentioned.

The aforementioned emails were placed in a folder marked SAVE, which actually contains 26 messages you've never seen, 23 of which would immediately increase your base paranoia by 87 percent.

There are upwards of 12,000 couples within 10 square miles of your house who had more measurable fun than you did in the last eight weeks, as evidenced by this graph (right). The red line is indicative of genuine laughter, the purple line represents long, meaningful stares, the blue line shows a water sport or plane ride, and the orange line depicts sunsets or sunrises enjoyed without irony or arguments.

Your current net approval rating is at 42 percent, revealing a divided house. If you look to your approval rating at this same time last year, it stood at 59 percent while, two years ago, it was at an all-time high of 81 percent, excepting that flu week when you wore the same sweatpants for 6 straight days. Your incessant, fever-stricken whining lowered your then approval to 54 percent (although sympathy conversely rose 13.6 percent in that same time frame). However, it's important to note that there is no rebound this time, according to polls with a margin of +/- 1. Across the board, you're less popular now than ever before.

According to a survey conducted last month, your partnership ranks as the second most doomed on your block, behind the couple who stand on their lawn and shriek at each other. Yours is statistically guaranteed to end three years sooner than that really attractive woman's, the one who recently moved in across the street and is home a mere 32 percent of the week. Of the 16 occasions you've peered through your blinds and noticed her walking to her car, she is on the phone with her boyfriend 53 percent of the time, and there's a 91.5 percent chance that it's serious.

The trend line shows that the odds of remaining in this current relationship hover steadily at 1 in 52, the very same chances of drawing the queen of hearts out of a deck of well-shuffled playing cards.

My procedures are not skewed toward your relationship failing, as I have a macro perspective on commitment and monogamy. By using quantitive polls and demographics—and after talking to numerous individuals who knew dozens of unhappy couples—I've accurately predicted exactly 50 out of 50 breakups this year. There is no reason to doubt my system. Valuations show that yours will meet a comparable end and that I will be right for the 51st consecutive time.

My breakup forecast shows you losing 35 of the albums you bought together at garage sales, leaving you with only 15, including Sting's fourth solo record, *Ten Summoner's Tales*, which neither of you really wanted. The album *does* contain the song "If I Ever Lose My Faith in You," which seems prescient in hindsight and which made it to #17 on the Billboard charts in 1993. There is a 97 percent chance you'll listen to the song at least 20 times.

Additionally, there is a 62.8 percent likelihood that your girlfriend will be dating somebody new within three months of your split. If this happens, there is an 84 percent chance that it's that new friend from the gym you keep hearing about (see photo).

Ultimately, please don't give me too much credit for this accumulated data. Although 0.0 percent of your mutual friends were willing to say anything, 93.9 percent of them saw this coming from the start.

IT'S NOT YOU,
IT'S QUANTITATIVE COST ANALYSIS.

by JOSH FREEDMAN

Susan, we need to talk. I've been doing a lot of thinking lately. About us. I really like you, but ever since we met in that econ class in college I knew there was something missing from how I felt: quantitative reasoning. We can say we love each other all we want, but I just can't trust it without the data. And after performing an in-depth cost-benefit analysis of our relationship, I just don't think this is working out.

Please know that this decision was not rash. In fact, it was anything but—it was completely devoid of emotion. I just made a series of quantitative calculations, culled from available OECD data on comparable families and conservative estimates of future likelihoods. I then assigned weights to various "feelings" based on importance, as judged by the relevant scholarly literature. From this, it was easy to determine that given all of the options available, the winning decision on both cost-effectiveness and comparative-effectiveness grounds was to see other people.

It's not you, it's me. Well, it's not me either: it's just common sense, given the nature of my utility function.

The calculations are fairly simple. At this point in my life, the opportunity cost of hanging out with you is fairly high. Sex with you grants me seventeen utils of pleasure, but I derive negative utils from all of the cuddling afterward and the excessive number of buttons on your blouse that makes it very difficult to maneuver in the heat of the moment. I also lose utils when you do that weird thing with your hands that you think is affectionate but feels almost like you're scratching me. Overall, I derive thirteen utils of pleasure on a typical Friday night with you, or fourteen if we watch *The Daily Show* as part of it (fifteen if they have a good guest on the show).

Meanwhile, I could be doing plenty of other things instead of spending time with you. For example, I could be drinking at The Irishman with a bunch of friends from work. I derive between 20 and 28 utils from hitting on drunk slutty girls at the bar. Since Jeff always buys most of the drinks anyway, the up-front pecuniary costs are low, and I have no potential negatives in terms of emotional investment. However, most of those girls don't laugh at my jokes, which drives down utils gained. Thus, I could get between 14 and 21 utils from a night out at the bar.

If you're looking for the kind of guy who's interested in maximizing the worst-off outcome regardless of potential gains—well, I'm not that guy. All you have to do is look at the probabilities and compare the feasible range of outcomes in terms of number of units of pleasure to see that we're going to have to call this relationship quits.

This may feel cold, but there's nothing cold about well-reasoned analysis.

Like all humans, I know I am fallible—and since I have a natural tendency to improperly discount the future, I have made sure to accurately determine present future value of costs and benefits. But even considering the diminishing marginal returns of hitting on the aforementioned drunk slutty girls, the numbers simply do not want us to be together.

I know this breakup might come as a bit of a shock to you, which I have also factored in. The disappointed look on your face costs me 5 utils of pleasure, but the knowledge that this is the right decision in the long term makes up for that. Additionally, I have included in my calculations the fact that as a courtesy I will have to pay for this dinner in its entirety, which, given the gender parity we have previously expressed in our relationship, would normally cost me only half that.

I want you to know that this decision isn't just for me—it's for you, too. I've done the calculations. There are plenty of eligible bachelors out there who are probably able to more vigorously, consistently, and knowledgeably have sexual intercourse with you. While the thought of you being with someone else causes me a substantial negative utility that makes me feel as though I am going to vomit, I know that in the aggregate everyone is better off, and therefore it is the right decision for us to make.

There's no need to try to persuade me otherwise, Susan. We just can't let our feelings get in the way of the math.

In the meantime, I need to get back home. My utility calculations tell me that the best thing I can do right now is strip down to my boxers, microwave a quesadilla, and watch a bunch of episodes of *The Wire*. It might seem strange and horribly unproductive, but it's not me—it's just my utility function.

PASSIVE-AGGRESSIVE VEGAN GROCERY CASHIER: A DAY IN THE LIFE.

by MEREDITH K. GRAY

6:30 A.M.

Awake to a bright and morally untroubling day. Waft into kitchen to prepare a healthy, animal-free breakfast. See that girlfriend (Jennifer) has cooked cream-of-tomato soup in my saucepan, and has left it in sink. Don't want to start fight. Instead, blend spirulina breakfast shake in blender for entirety of time in shower.

7:30 A.M.

Put PETA I AM NOT A NUGGET T-shirt on under work polo. I know I've made a small difference.

8:15 A.M.–8:25 A.M.

After leaving questionably sarcastic note for Jennifer, drive to work. Tailgate Durango with CARNIVORE sticker. Feel he noticed: small victory. Arrive at work. Clock in. Intentionally snub butchers' department; give them the finger with hands in pockets.

9:20 A.M.

Fellow cashier (Brandi) asks for price on eggs. "The price is too high," I say. "Too high." She is so moved by my answer, she does not consult me for price checks for rest of day.

10:25 A.M.

Get poultry drippings on shirt from raw chicken at checkout. Consider changing into extra work shirt, but decide not to. Fluids will be Pink Badge of Sacrifice. Brandi tells me I have chicken blood on my shirt. "But not on my hands," I say.

11:00 A.M.

Overcharge woman buying Jell-O.

11:15 A.M.

Lunch break. Eat bagel with peanut butter sprinkled with texturized vegetable protein. Brandi sits nearby, eating turkey sandwich. Stomach turns. She asks if she should eat elsewhere. I say, "No, I just won't breathe through my nose." After meal, go to loading dock and smoke cigarette to clear air of turkey smell.

11:45 A.M.

Return from lunch break. Remove Burt's Bees products from display next to register. Manager complains. Tell her I'm sorry, that from now on I will be more accepting of the exploitation of bees. She asks me to work every Saturday for the month. I accept, interested to see how many pork products are bought on Sabbath. Will make great entry in journal.

12:50 P.M.

Customer comments on GO VEG! sticker, which is on my water bottle under counter. I give short discourse on Marxist view of man-v.-animal struggle, especially as it pertains to bovine lactation exploitation. I "accidentally" spill his container of feta on floor. He informs me he will no longer shop here. I congratulate his grass-roots activism against the grocery industry.

1:30 P.M.

Ask customer if she wants paper or plastic. Add, "Or a coronary," as I cough into hand. Feel energized about standing up for beliefs.

2:55 P.M.

Brandi asks if I am mad about the sandwich incident. I say no, but know she knows I'm mad. Continue covert glaring toward her register.

3:10 P.M.

Smoke break. Co-worker (Dave) says, "I'm surprised you do that." "Well, being vegan isn't for everyone," I counter. Note he must be jealous of my self-control.

4:00 P.M.

Receive call from Jennifer. Asks if I can pick up birth-control prescription. I begin to mention the evils of hormone harvesting from horses, but refrain. Decide to "forget" to go to pharmacy.

4:30 P.M.

Clock out. Grab wheat-grass smoothie for drive home. Accidentally let shopping carts roll into butcher's car. Oops.

4:45 P.M.–6:00 P.M.

Confrontation with Jennifer over birth control. She says pills are
"synthetic" hormones. I say the only thing synthetic are my shoes—no
leather here! I refuse to have intercourse until a non-latex-based,
nonhormonal birth-control method is established. Jennifer rummages
through vegetable crisper, retires to bedroom. I believe she is beginning
to see the light.

7:45 P.M.

Leaf through PETA catalog (new hemp shoes!), eat tofu stir-fry. Decide
not to brush teeth after eating as I usually do to accommodate Jennifer's
soy sensitivity. Give her sloppy kiss when she emerges from bedroom.
Swear that resulting hives are from a built-up Midwestern resistance
to healthful, non-meat alternatives. She begins to cry. Finally, a
breakthrough.

10:20 P.M.

Read *Vegan Delights* cookbook in bed, fall asleep on goose-down pillows
Jennifer put on bed. Could go to closet and get fiberfill one, but don't.
Will blame Jennifer forever if ideological tenets are damaged by night of
fluffy respite. Pledge to record this in journal tomorrow.

MIDDLE MANAGER'S OATH.

by CHRISTOPHER MAH

(To be recited by corporate managers and senior managers each morning while looking in a full-length mirror, topless, and flexing their biceps.)

- - - -

I will empower my team to find their own solutions to those problems, which I do not want to deal with myself.

I will be decisive in making crucial decisions that I do not trust my team enough to make themselves.

I will evangelize the use of data-driven decision-making because my gut tells me it's the right thing to do.

I will take expense reports extremely seriously, much more seriously than the HR Code of Conduct, which does not apply to me.

Because I have no life outside of work, I will expect the same of my team.

I will take credit for any project I named.

If an important executive disagrees with something I say, I will apologize for my choice of words and then rephrase it in a way that makes it seem like we were actually in agreement all along.

I will never contradict myself. I will sometimes contradict myself. I will often contradict you, usually in front of your clients, and then pretend to take a call on my phone while you handle damage control.

Asking employees to document and submit a log of their hourly activities does not count as busy work so long as I preface it by saying, "This is not intended to be busy work."

I will drop names. I will drop them like they're hot.

I believe that business is best done in person, which is why I never read important emails.

One of my opinions is worth three of your facts.

I will reward members of my team for good work with praise and other non-monetary forms of positive reinforcement. Examples of good work include responding to emails on weekends, agreeing with something I say in large group meetings, and belonging to a chapter of the same national fraternity as the one I was in.

I will challenge my team to solve the problems I unnecessarily created for them.

Every member of my team is unique and indispensable, so I will make it virtually impossible for them to be transferred or promoted.

The fact that I have an MBA from a third-tier university means that I can use terms like "market valuation," "expected yield," and "externality," but rarely ever in the correct context.

I will lead my team, mostly through the elaborate maze of hoops I jump through while chasing a fictitious promotion that exists only so that upper management can keep me motivated to continue working ninety-hour weeks.

I will be reliably late to meetings which I myself called and tagged on your calendar as "urgent," and then need to leave early, preventing anything from being accomplished.

Jargon is not meaningless as long as it is strategic, measurable, and scalable.

I will make at least one effort per month to engage my direct reports on a more personal level, whether that means talking about sports, asking about their children, or telling them about my marital problems. The topic is not important, so long as I have demonstrated that I am not too proud to stoop down to their level for a few seconds.

I will become diabolically drunk with the slightest sip of power.

I believe my female employees deserve as much recognition as my male employees, which is why every time I compliment a male employee on his intelligence, I also compliment a female employee on her looks.

I will motivate my team to victory like a surgeon leading his soldiers into the championship game. When I have no idea what I am talking about, I will use an awkwardly worded simile, which I will refer to as a metaphor.

I will form a super-exclusive club with other middle managers where we only eat lunch with each other, share all sorts of inside jokes, require an elaborate secret handshake to enter each other's offices, and wear matching rings, which, when touched together, turn us into a single, giant super-manager with unlimited budget-approval powers.

But if a promotion opens up, I will stab them in the back in a heartbeat.

I WOULD LIKE TO BE POPE.

by JOHN ORIVED

Dear sir or madam,

I am writing to apply for the position of Pope. I recently received my
Bachelor of Arts, or "artium baccalaureus," from Dartmouth College,
with a major concentration in Theatre Studies and a minor concentration
in Computer Science. While I have been focusing on the technology
and financial sectors, I have recently decided to widen my job search to
include top nonprofits, such as your organization. I became aware of the
availability of the position of Pope through the Dartmouth listserv; I am
greatly impressed by the achievements of The Catholic Church and share
many of its goals. I believe my qualifications and outlook make me a
unique and interesting candidate for Pope, and I would be enthusiastic to
grow with The Catholic Church.

Over the past four years, I have worked tirelessly to receive the
kind of well-rounded education that is indispensible to today's leaders,
whether in the boardroom, the operating room, or the Vatican. My
thesis project, a musical *King Lear* that took place entirely on Facebook,
integrated my chosen areas of study, including Advanced Shakespeare,

Social Media and Society, and Twentieth Century History of Latin Jazz. As social chair of my fraternity, AXA, I not only increased the attendance of our weekly No-Pants Parties by 30 percent, I successfully persuaded the Dartmouth Disciplinary Council to permit AXA to conduct internal reviews of alleged incidents of sexual harassment and bullying. I am a problem solver.

While I have never studied Catholicism per se, I have several credits in World Religions, and, as the intern supervisor at the prominent, Oakland law firm of Russ, Davies & Chalmers will confirm, I am a quick study. Additionally, I have noted your organization's expanding client base in South America. This is an area in which I am well versed, after spending an entire semester in Buenos Aires, where I became intimately acquainted with the people, their food, and their culture. Well-traveled and a man of the world, I think my Spanish language skills *hablar* for themselves.

As your website notes, the role of Pope includes "Guiding the College of Cardinals, and the masses." Through my participation in the Freshman Buddy Program, I have helped many younger students through difficult situations, including homesickness and mono. I feel like it is important to give back, a value I believe any organization would appreciate in their Pope.

As an excellent student with advanced people skills and an exciting résumé, with a desire to be part of a challenging, energetic, and reputable organization, I will be a valuable addition to The Catholic Church as your new Pope.

While I am focusing my employment search in the San Francisco Bay Area, I am open to a discussion of relocation.

I thank you in advance for your consideration,
John Ortved

WHY THERE AREN'T MANY RIGHT-WING OBSERVATIONAL COMEDIANS.

by TEDDY WAYNE

You ever see a roomful of old white guys trying to dance? They're bumping along out of rhythm to some corny '50s song in their tuxedoes, like three feet away from their wives, and you're just like, "Yes—that's exactly what respectable nightlife socializing should be."

- - - -

I'm in the supermarket checkout the other day, and this woman is taking forever to pay—with her checkbook, of course. So I lean over and say, "Hey, lady, you know what we're all thinking when you pay by check? That you're not reaping any potential benefits from a cash-back or frequent-flyer credit card." I mean, how stupid can you be not to know that most major cards give triple miles for supermarket or drugstore purchases? Am I right, people?

- - - -

My wife complains like it's her job. About out-of-control government spending and affirmative action. And I totally agree with her. She's a spokeswoman for Rick Santorum.

- - - -

The other day, on a flight, I open up my package of peanuts, and there are *five* peanuts inside. I ask the flight attendant if there's a mistake, and she says it's a cost-cutting procedure to help save the airline from bankruptcy. I go, "Oh, yeah? You want an idea for another 'cost-cutting procedure'? How 'bout taking a stand against the pilots' union and raising the retirement age to sixty-five from the current sixty so the 401(k)s aren't depleted and the average middle-to-upper-class passenger doesn't foot the bill?" Boo-ya!

- - - -

I once had this real tight-ass boss who constantly yelled at all his employees for slacking off. For our Christmas bonuses, he gave us tube socks. *Tube socks.* And, by saving money, he was able to hire new, better employees the next year, fire us, and improve profit margins. That man knew how to run a fiscally responsible company.

- - - -

The other night my wife and I are watching *Hannity & Colmes*, and she goes, "I'm cold—let's turn up the heat." So I say, "Just put on a sweater." And she gives me this look that's like, *No missionary sex in the marital interest of procreation for you!* And I'm thinking, "Man, if only the pansy liberals let the military flex a little more muscle in the Middle East and force an effective European coalition, we might be able to dissolve the OPEC terrorists, gain some leverage over oil prices, and avert domestic crises like this." The fellas know what I mean!

- - - -

You guys seen *Brokeback Mountain*? I actually thought it could've been a good movie. If one of the guys were a woman. And they were married. And practicing Christians. And they didn't outsource the directing to Taiwan.

- - - -

Where are you folks from? Paris? Really? *Voulez-vous coucher avec moi ce soir*? Ha ha, just kidding, *madame*. But get out of my face. Seriously. You make me sick.

Response to *On the Implausibility of the*
Death Star's Trash Compactor #4

⁂

From: Tim Streisel
Date: Thu, Feb 23, 2012
Re: Death Star Garbage Compactor

Not that I am authorized to speak for the Empire, or his
Imperial Majesty, George Lucas ... but I would like to offer
rebuttal to the points made in your argument about the
plausibility of the trash compactors on the Death Star.

ISSUE NO. 1 deals with the vent that Princess Leia finds.
You argue that there is no reason to vent the stench of
rotting material in such a manner. I remind you that the
vent leads to the detention blocks, and could have been
installed out of pure spite, in an attempt to make the
inmates' lives just that much more uncomfortable. The
Empire was big on spite, ya know.

ISSUE NO. 2 assumes that compaction efficiency is the
priority. However, if the priority is speed of the compaction
cycle, then movable opposing walls make sense.

ISSUE NO. 3: Many types of equipment use linkages that
vary the speed/force through the motion cycle. It seems that
the compactor walls could have that type of linkage, as the
force needed for compaction would grow as the walls move
inward and more trash is compacted. The slowing down of
the compactor you see may very well been designed into

the system. I notice that the compactor never jammed or stopped till R2 halted it.

ISSUE NO. 4: Remember that R2 did indeed halt the compaction cycle, so we have no way of knowing if the other two walls or ceiling/floor would move as the next stage of the cycle. More car crushers work with a two- or three-stage cycle like that.

ISSUE NO. 5: The design/size of the floor is never shown, but based on what is shown when Luke is pulled under the water, the case can be made about the floor being a platform that is smaller than the area of the room. It is possible that all refuse, once compacted, is allowed to sink to the bottom of the pool of water for disposal or processing. If designed properly, any piece small enough to pass through the gap between wall and floor would be small enough for downstream processing equipment to handle.

ISSUE NO. 6: The Death Star is a military base. One system is more reliable and uses less manpower to operate and maintain than two. For a civilian installation, where quality of life is the priority, separate systems make sense, but not for a military one.

ISSUE NO. 7: The Empire obviously could care less for the distinction between organic and inorganic waste. Its primary sanitation objective is to remove any and all waste from the facility. You also assume that the Empire actually put the worm into the system. It could very well be a product of some larva that was discarded and pupated in the waste system. This is not unheard of here on Earth.

ISSUE NO. 8: Sanitation on ships equals recourses and manpower to run them, for little or no gain over simply jettisoning garbage. If the Empire had even the slightest glimmer of a ecological movement in its ranks, it would be very simple to arrange the jettisoned garbage into a decaying orbit around a star.

ISSUE NO. 9: The Death Star would surely make a tremendous amount of waste. And true, space is infinite. But manpower is not. Compacting the trash means fewer jettison cycles. That would also be the reason for speed to be the priority for the operation of the compactors (hence the two moving walls) rather than compaction efficiency. The unknown question is whether or not operating/maintaining the compactors uses less manpower than running more jettison cycles.

As far as creating hassles for the Empire ... You rebel scum!

Go Empire!

Tim Streisel
Imperial (no kidding), Missouri

OUR DAUGHTER ISN'T A SELFISH BRAT; YOUR SON JUST HASN'T READ *ATLAS SHRUGGED*.

by ERIC HAGUE

I'd like to start by saying that I don't get into belligerent shouting matches at the playground very often. The Tot Lot, by its very nature, can be an extremely volatile place— a veritable powder keg of different and sometimes contradictory parenting styles—and this fact alone is usually enough to keep everyone, parents and tots alike, acting as courteous and deferential as possible. The argument we had earlier today didn't need to happen, and I want you to know, above all else, that I'm deeply sorry that things got so wildly, publicly out of hand.

Now let me explain why your son was wrong.

When little Aiden toddled up our daughter Johanna and asked to play with her Elmo ball, he was, admittedly, very sweet and polite. I think his exact words were, "Have a ball, peas [*sic*]?" And I'm sure you were very proud of him for using his manners.

To be sure, I was equally proud when Johanna yelled, "No! Looter!" right in his looter face, and then only marginally less proud when she sort of shoved him.

The thing is, in this family we take the philosophies of Ayn Rand seriously. We conspicuously reward ourselves for our own hard work, we never give to charity, and we only pay our taxes very, very begrudgingly.

Since the day Johanna was born, we've worked to indoctrinate her into the truth of Objectivism. Every night we read to her from the illustrated, unabridged edition of *Atlas Shrugged*—glossing over all the hard-core sex parts, mind you, but dwelling pretty thoroughly on the stuff about being proud of what you've earned and not letting James Taggart–types bring you down. For a long time we were convinced that our efforts to free her mind were for naught, but recently, as we've started socializing her a little bit, we've been delighted to find that she is completely antipathetic to the concept of sharing. As parents, we couldn't have asked for a better daughter.

That's why, when Johanna then began berating your son, accusing him of trying to coerce from her a moral sanction of his theft of the fruit of her labor, in as many words, I kind of egged her on. Even when Aiden started crying.

You see, that Elmo ball was Johanna's reward for consistently using the potty this past week. She wasn't given the ball simply because she'd demonstrated an exceptional need for it—she earned it. And from the way Aiden's pants sagged as he tried in vain to run away from our daughter, it was clear that he wasn't anywhere close to deserving that kind of remuneration. By so much as allowing Johanna to share her toy with him, we'd be undermining her appreciation of one of life's most important lessons: you should never feel guilty about your abilities. Including your ability to repeatedly peg a fellow toddler with your Elmo ball as he sobs for mercy.

Look, imagine what would happen if we were to enact some sort of potty-training Equalization of Opportunity Act in which we regularized the distribution all of Johanna's and Aiden's potty chart stickers.

Suddenly it would seem as if Aiden had earned the right to wear big-boy underpants, and within minutes you'd have a Taggart Tunnelesque catastrophe on your hands, if you follow me.

Johanna shouldn't be burdened with supplying playthings for every bed-wetting moocher she happens to meet. If you saw Johanna, her knees buckling, her arms trembling but still trying to hold aloft the collective weight of an entire Tot Lot's worth of Elmo balls with the last of her strength, what would you tell her to do?

To shrug. Just like we've instructed her to do if Child Protective Services or some other agent of the People's State of America ever asks her about what we're teaching her.

After all, we've managed to raise a bright, self-reliant girl who achieves her goals by means of incentive and ratiocination and never— or very rarely—through the corrupt syllogism of force. We know, despite what you and a number of other parents we've met have said—as they carried their whimpering little social parasites away—that Johanna's defiant, quasi-bellicose nature only superficially resembles that of an out-of-control toddler, and in truth posits her as more of a latter-day Dagny Taggart than any kind of *enfant terrible*.

Yes, she's blossomed into everything we ever hoped or post-hoc rationalized she would. In our house we no longer say, "Who is John Galt?" Instead we say, "Who's our little princess?"

TOTO'S "AFRICA" BY ERNEST HEMINGWAY.

by ANTHONY SAMS

At the airport the young man heard far-off drums echoing in the night. He imagined the young woman in the plane sitting still, hearing whispers of a quiet conversation near the rear of the fuselage. He glanced down at his father's wristwatch—12:30. The flight was on time.

The plane's wings were moonlit and reflected the stars. The moonlight had guided him there, toward this salvation. He had stopped an older man along the way, hoping to find some long-forgotten words, or perhaps an ancient melody, for such an occasion. The old man had said nothing at first, and instead stared cryptically into the sodden earth. Then he raised his head and turned slowly.

"Hurry, boy. It's waiting there for you," the old man had said.

The plane was almost gliding. The young man looked at the wristwatch again. His head spun from whiskey and soda. She was a damned nice woman. It would take a lot to drag him away from her. It was unlikely that a hundred men or more could ever do such a thing. The air, now thick and moist, seemed to carry rain again. He blessed the rains of Africa. They were the only thing left to bless in this forsaken place, he thought—at least until she set foot on the continent. They were going to take some time to do the things they never had.

He stood on the tarmac and watched as the plane came in for its landing. He heard the sound of wild dogs crying out into the night. The man thought the dogs sounded desperate, perhaps having grown restless and longing for some company. He knew the feeling. The crying of the dogs reminded him that he would need to do what he knew was right now that she was here. Of this he was as certain as Kilimanjaro rising like Olympus above the Serengeti. He had traveled and sought to cure what was deep inside him, what frightened him of himself.

The plane landed and stopped. He hurried. She would be waiting there for him.

HALL AND OATES AND ROSENCRANTZ AND GUILDENSTERN.

by JOHN K. PECK

ACT II, SCENE II

Enter KING CLAUDIUS, QUEEN GERTRUDE, ROSENCRANTZ, GUILDENSTERN, HALL, OATES, *and Attendants.*

KING CLAUDIUS

Welcome, gentlemen; our urgent need did provoke
Our hasty sending.

ROSENCRANTZ

Both your majesties
Might, by the sovereign power you have of us,
Put your dread pleasures more into command
Than to entreaty.

GUILDENSTERN

But we four obey,

And here give up ourselves to be commanded.

HALL

You've got to know
What my head overlooks
The senses will show to my heart;
When it's watching for lies
You can't escape my
Private Eyes.

OATES
(*silent*)

(*long pause*)

KING CLAUDIUS
(*clears throat*)

That will be all.

QUEEN GERTRUDE

Ay, amen!

Exeunt KING CLAUDIUS, ROSENCRANTZ, GUILDENSTERN, *and* Attendants.

QUEEN GERTRUDE
(*places her hand on HALL's chest*)
Stay, you lion-maned pair, tell me
Of your distant City of Brotherly Love,
That we may, as they say, get to know

The heft and measure of each other's thoughts.

HALL
I can't go for that.

OATES
No can do.

HALL
I can't go for that, can't go for that, can't go for that.

Enter SAXOPHONIST; QUEEN GERTRUDE *flees*.

- - - -

ACT II, SCENE III

Enter HAMLET, ROSENCRANTZ, GUILDENSTERN, HALL, *and* OATES.

HAMLET
My excellent good friends! How do ye four?

ROSENCRANTZ
As the indifferent children of the earth.

GUILDENSTERN
Happy, in that we are not over-happy;
On fortune's cap we are not the very button.

HALL

Mmmm, yeah. Mmmm, yeah, hey.

OATES

(*silent*)

HAMLET

There is a kind of confession in your looks
Which your modesties have not craft enough to colour:
I know the good king and queen have sent for you.

HALL

Don't you know
That it's wrong to take
What he's giving you;
You can get along
If you try to be strong
But you'll never be strong.

HAMLET

(*long pause*)

I ... sure.
Now, make haste to the king's chamber,
To his chamber, go!

Exeunt ROSENCRANTZ, GUILDENSTERN, *and* HALL.

HAMLET (CONT.)

Stay, dusky Oates, for your silence doth seem
The still surface of the deepest waters, and I lack gall

To make oppression bitter for this tyrant,
This remorseless, treacherous, lecherous, kindless villain!
O, vengeance!

OATES

Vengeance, whoa-oh.

HAMLET

Prompted to my revenge by heaven and hell,
I fall a-cursing, like a very drab, a scullion!

OATES

A scullion, woo, scullion, whoa-oh.

HAMLET

Abuse me to damn me, but I'll have grounds
More relative than this: the play's the thing
Wherein I'll catch the conscience—

OATES

Conscience, whoa, conscience, whoa-oh.

OATES *vamps for eight more minutes*; HAMLET *waits awkwardly.*

- - - -

ACT III, SCENE II

Danish march. A flourish. Enter HAMLET, KING CLAUDIUS, QUEEN
GERTRUDE, POLONIUS, ROSENCRANTZ, GUILDENSTERN,

HALL, OATES, *and others.*

HAMLET

They are coming to the play; I must be idle:
Get you a place. Where be Ophelia? My own person,
Like the sun, doth daily rise to greet her.

HALL

I wouldn't if I were you,
I know what she can do,
She's deadly, man, she could really rip your world apart.
Mind over matter, ooh, the beauty is there,
But a beast is in the heart.

OATES
(silent)

HAMLET
(clears throat)
Go, bid the players make ready.

ROSENCRANTZ *and* GUILDENSTERN
We will, my lord.

Exeunt ROSENCRANTZ *and* GUILDENSTERN. *Enter* OPHELIA.

OATES
Whoa-oh, here she comes.

HALL

Watch out boy, she'll chew you up.

OATES

Whoa-oh, here she comes.

HALL

She's a maneater.

HAMLET

Let the show begin!

Enter a dozen SAXOPHONISTS.

KING CLAUDIUS

Gods, no! Give me some light: away!

Exeunt all.

- - - -

ACT IV, SCENE VII

HALL *and* OATES *stand graveside. Enter* LAERTES.

LAERTES

What news? Hast seen Ophelia this day?

HALL

Everybody's high on consolation,

Everybody's trying to tell me what's right for me, yeah,
My daddy tried to bore me with a sermon,
But it's plain to see that they can't comfort me.

LAERTES

Come, what news, knave? Out with it!

HALL

Sorry, Charlie, for the imposition,
I think I've got it, got it, I've got the strength to carry on, yeah.
I need a drink and a quick decision,
Now it's up to me, ooh, what will be.

LAERTES

Come, you devils! Out, out with it!

HALL

She's gone.

OATES

She's gone.

HALL

Oh, I, oh, I,
I'd better learn how to face it.
She's gone.

OATES

She's gone.

HALL

Oh, I, oh, I,
I pay the devil to replace her.
She's gone.

Enter SAXOPHONIST, *playing.*

HALL

She's gone.

OATES

She's gone.

HALL, OATES, *and* SAXOPHONIST *continue thusly for sixteen minutes;*
LAERTES *waits awkwardly.*

- - - -

ACT V, SCENE II

Enter FORTINBRAS, HORATIO, ENGLISH AMBASSADORS,
and others.

PRINCE FORTINBRAS

This quarry cries on havoc. O proud death,
What feast is toward in thine eternal cell,
That thou so many princes at a shot
So bloodily hast struck?

FIRST AMBASSADOR

The sight is dismal;
And our affairs from England come too late:
The ears are senseless that should give us hearing,
To tell him his commandment is fulfill'd,
That Rosencrantz and Guildenstern and Hall and Oates are dead:
Where should we have our thanks?

HORATIO

(distraught)

Not from his mouth,
Had it the ability of life to thank you:
He never gave commandment for their death.

FIRST AMBASSADOR

The saxophonists, too, are rightly hanged.

HORATIO

Rejoice! Prepare the table for feasting!

A heavy blues-soul march. Exeunt, bearing the dead bodies.

CURTAIN.

BONO GIVES THE RUSH-HOUR TRAFFIC REPORT.

by ALYSSA LANG

Listen, everybody. Listen up. There's an epidemic in this country.
An epidemic of waiting. An epidemic of sitting. In traffic.

There are people waiting in line. Day after bloody day. People.
Wanting to go home. People. Sick. And tired.

Of waiting.

People. Waiting for the government to fix the problems of
the people. People. Waiting for a sign. For a sign that says END
CONSTRUCTION ZONE!

Waiting.

To see the flashing lights. In the distance. Under a blood-red sky.
The flashing lights that say, "I've passed the three-car pileup on the
westbound turnpike." I see people. Sitting in their cars. Burning their
fossil fuels. Their transmissions. I-DL-ING! On the expressway. Sitting.
On I-95.

Waiting.

You want to know what I see? A car fire on Route 422? A stalled
vehicle blocking the right lane on the A.C. Expressway? No. I see an

overturned tractor-trailer on 76. Spilling its toxic load. Poisoning the innocent commuters. And I see people. People looking down the barrel of a ten. Mile. Delay.

People.

They want to know. When will this madness end? How long until I reach my exit? How long will the U.S. government, and its hired contractors, be repaving Interstate 476? It has to end. And if we don't do something about it our children are gonna suffer. And our children's children. And our children's children's children. And our children's children's children's children.

People.

Waiting.

Back to you, Jim.

THE MAGIC 8 BALL AMENDED BY MY MOTHER FOR MY MIDDLE-SCHOOL YEARS.

by KATE HAHN

Very doubtful. But you brought that on yourself.

As I see it, yes. But when was the last time you cared what I thought?

My sources say yes. And they have no reason to lie about seeing you at the mall in the middle of a school day

It is decidedly so. I just know.

Outlook good. Let's see how long that lasts.

Outlook not so good. See?

Better not tell you now. You seem upset and I'm afraid you might do something irrational. At least that's what *Time* magazine says about teenagers.

Signs point to yes. The incense, for one. How stupid do you think I am?

Don't count on it. Or on much else if you keep going the way you're going.

Yes—definitely. Oh wait, I thought that was your sister holding the ball. For you, no.

Reply hazy. Try again when I'm off the phone with my boyfriend.

Concentrate and ask again. I can't abide poor grammar.

My reply is no. Crying won't change things.

Ask again later. Maybe in twenty years, when you'll understand what you put me through.

You may rely on it. Let's just hope "it" can rely on you, too. Poor "it."

Yes. As long as an adult is present and your grades are good. So I guess it's actually no.

Most likely. Especially if your friends are already doing it.

Cannot predict now. But, if your past behavior is any indication, the results will include my picking you up at the police station at 4 a.m.

It is certain. Everyone blames the mother.

THE FOUR-YEAR-OLD'S WORKDAY.

by ROSS MURRAY

8:55 A.M.

Arrive at office. Hang jacket on sunshine-shaped hook with name on it.
Put snack in cubbyhole. Sing "Good Morning" song with co-workers.

9:04 A.M.

Forward hilarious e-mail to everyone in address book. Subject line:
"Poo-poo."

9:10 A.M.

Take spreadsheets out of *Star Wars* backpack. Stretch out on floor and
begin making notations with crayon.

9:15 A.M.

Drink juice box.

9:25 A.M.

Spend hour lining up office supplies on desk in perfect straight line.
Toy with idea of sorting them by color but get distracted by imaginary

conversation between stapler and three-hole punch. Complicated scenario ensues involving a lion, a puppy, and the mommy Hi-Liter kissing the daddy Hi-Liter.

10:40 A.M.

Randy from accounting drops by and "borrows" pen with the springy pink feather on top. Grab pen back. Scream in each other's faces until Randy takes a swing with copy of Needs-Assessment Analysis. Supervisor intervenes and sends Randy to the smoke room for a time-out.

11:05 A.M.

Intend to begin debugging online program for cross-referencing customer demographics. Get caught up in Polly Pocket website instead.

12:00 P.M.

Lunch. Trade PB&J for tuna with Jerry from human resources. Friendly banter about who could take who in a fight: the Poky Little Puppy or the Cat in the Hat. Notice Donna is wearing *Finding Nemo* T-shirt for fourth straight day.

1:00 P.M.

Write up statistical profile of user satisfaction based on regional trends. Entitle report "I Like Flowers."

1:30 P.M.

Naptime.

2:12 P.M.

Staff meeting proves unproductive due to constant requests to go pee.

2:40 P.M.

Telephone headquarters to discuss department budget for upcoming fiscal year. While talking, draw picture of house. Feel special pride in the way the smoke spirals out of chimney. Tape picture to wall next to trophy for company T-ball championship.

3:00 P.M.

Attend mandatory Employees' Committee workshop entitled "Ear Infections Are EVERYBODY'S Business." Session comes to abrupt halt when VP of finance jams eraser up nose.

3:30 P.M.

E-mail from director of marketing: "I'm not accusing anyone but my blankie was in the copy room and now it's not. I hope whoever 'accidentally' took it will please return it, no questions asked. Otherwise I'm telling."

4:05 P.M.

Ask Marco in adjoining cubicle to stop making "vroom vroom" noises when he moves the mouse.

4:45 P.M.

Try to duck out early, thus avoiding mandatory singing of "Clean-up" song with co-workers. Busted by supervisor, who announces that no one is leaving until everyone is sitting quietly.

4:55 P.M.

Retrieve jacket from hook. Supervisor helps with zipper. Wave bye-bye to Cheryl at the front desk. Step into elevator. Press all the buttons.

SPARKNOTES: *GOODNIGHT MOON*.

by SEAN WALSH

CONTEXT

America after the Great War was full of economic prosperity and social upheaval. Margaret Wise Brown, renowned children's book author, made it her life's goal to both comfort the youth of the era and expose the flaws of human advancement through her didactic work. In *Goodnight Moon*, Brown explores the relationship between a young bunny and his material possessions set against the backdrop of the Cold War. The book was met with critical and commercial success. Margaret Wise Brown's work, which has been translated into countless languages and has sold over 40 million copies, still resonates with children's librarians and counter-culture revolutionaries for its duality as good-natured poetry and allegory of human alienation.

PLOT OVERVIEW

A bunny says goodnight to the moon and other things.

SUMMARY/ANALYSIS

The book opens as a young bunny prepares for sleep in his bedroom. The
first half of Brown's magnum opus is entirely devoted to the contents
of "the great green room." As symbolic items such as a "balloon" and a
"telephone" are described, our protagonist bunny, oppressively tucked
into bed, resists the confines of sleep. Brown gives particular attention
to a large number of animals that populate the room: "two kittens with
mittens" and a "little mouse." The room also contains a picture of a
"cow jumping over a moon" and "bears on chairs." Here, Brown twists
our preconceptions of settings—where the internal now is wild, but the
external ("the moon" and "the stars") serene. The room full of raging
wildlife mirrors the little bunny's desire to throw off his sheets and play.

At the midpoint of her Homeric epic, Brown reveals an antagonist:
"a quiet old lady whispering hush." The bunny, first enthralled by
the items, now must face an authority figure desiring quiet in the
wild. Succumbing to his Oedipal desire to please his maternal figure,
the bunny starts to settle and go to bed. Then, in a process of self-
actualization, the young bunny says goodnight to everything both in and
out of the room. The climax is realized when the bunny says goodnight
to the "old woman who says hush," thereby making his amends and
completing his quixotic journey to rid himself of his surroundings. In the
denouement, the bunny turns his attention to the outer world in ways
not unlike Tom Joad in *The Grapes of Wrath*. At peace with the loss of his
maternal authority figure, the young bunny says goodnight to the moon,
whose presence loomed throughout the narrative.

THEMES

Materialism in American Culture — The post–World War II economic
boom figures heavily in Brown's sharp critique of newfound prosperity.
A careful Marxist examination might suggest a strong anti-capitalist

sentiment. She carefully chooses to set the story in a *"green* room." While surely the overly materialized room of the bunny excites and overwhelms his senses and severs his relationships, Brown finds fault more in our inability to extricate ourselves from the clutches of capitalism—(think Thoreau)—than in the systemic trappings of the American economic system. [See note on *The Red Balloon.*] However, the title of the book put in the context of the impending space race gives credence to Brown's polemic warning that we—perhaps both Russians and Americans—should say "goodnight moon" and focus our attention on rebuilding relationships.

Search for the Masculine Self — As in many other Bildungsromans, e.g., *The Catcher in the Rye* and *A Separate Peace*, Brown adopts the voice of a young male protagonist trying to find himself. While lacking the acerbic wit of Holden Caulfield and the taut homoeroticism of Finny and Gene, the young bunny's voice is, at the same time, quite powerful. He is dismissive of the world. His complete nihilism and rejection of his parents are ripe precursors to the era to come (1950s).

SYMBOLS

The Moon — The moon in this piece acts as a traditionally feminine sign. Here, the bunny's final "goodnight moon" demonstrates his completion of his rite of passage and his development into a full man bunny. The moon, which visually appears on every page, grows larger and more pronounced—it is a chanting feminine voice, haunting and disturbing his world. Just as he must overcome his sexual desire for the woman who says "hush," the bunny must resist the impending femininity outside of his safe confines. In Queer Theory, the bunny's final admonishment—"goodnight noises everywhere"—represents his full-on embrace of a heteronormative lifestyle and a rejection of his "deviant" thoughts, probably about the kittens with the mittens.

The Red Balloon — A subtle, yet appropriate reference to communism. The bunny's desire to rid himself of the balloon's presence by saying goodnight enforces Brown's ardent McCarthy-era beliefs. This symbol is only more fully realized in the unwatchable film of the same name and in the hit song "99 Luftballons" by Nena.

POSSIBLE ESSAY QUESTIONS

1. Analyze the scene in which the bunny says goodnight to the lighthouse in relationship to the rest of the book. Cite textual evidence whenever possible.

2. Compare and contrast *Goodnight Moon* with *The Sun Also Rises*. Whose sentences are simpler: Brown's or Hemingway's?

3. What have you said goodnight to? Analyze what that says about you. Try not to cry.

AMERICA: A REVIEW.

by MEGAN AMRAM

How to begin this review? Few countries that debuted in the 1700s have been as controversial or long running (it's into its 237th season now) as *America*. It may not have the staying power of perennial favorites such as *China* or the credibility of indie darlings such as *Finland*, but *America* has proven that it can at least make some cultural impact. It's not the best, but hey, they can't all be *Louie*.

America was originally a spin-off of the long-running *England*. Airing from the 1776–77 season through today, *America* focuses on a small ensemble of white people using things in the ground to become rich or kill brown people. A sprawling dramedy, it combines all of the loose plot points of a Tyler Perry sitcom with all the fun of being white.

It has widely focused on the themes of war, freedom, sitting, Fenway Park, maps, the one true Christian god, rugs, pregnancy tits, *Vice* magazine, butterfaces, coal, butterdicks, "Where's the Beef?," Chicago, Larry Flynt, colonialism, Terri Schiavo, NBC single-camera sitcoms, toddlers, suicide pacts, Atari, penny farthing bicycles, SpaghettiO's (Cool Ranch flavor), tiny dolls, the TLC show *Sister Wives*, H1N1, television, and genocide. It has some unique perspective every once in awhile, but honestly, *America* can be super derivative. Most of the stories have already been on *The Simpsons*.

A lot of episodes in *America* don't really hold up. Slavery? Parachute pants? White slavery? It just feels really overdone now. Among the most memorable episodes are "The Civil War," "Texas," "World War" (a two-parter), and "Black President."

Some of the storylines are also a bit of a stretch. Are they really expecting us to believe that they killed all the Indians and that all those Indians did to deserve it was invent diabetes?! And *come on*—that stuff in the 9/11 episode could not have happened without someone working on the inside. That makes no sense. "9/11" jumped the shark. Hard.

It's been on so long that no one wants to comment on the OBVIOUS PLOT HOLES. Such awful continuity. Like, how could it be explained that in season 170, George H. W. Bush fathered a mentally disabled son, but then in season 225, that son became president?! Really terrible continuity. I would like to point out that I do appreciate a recent callback to earlier plots. Around seasons 174–184, some of the antifeminist and sexist storylines were put on the backburner, but it's nice that we've seen a resurgence in this last season.

America has time and time again proved itself as a launching ground for young starlets. It's fun seeing people before they became huge stars, like John Ritter, Stella McCartney, Theodore "Ted" Kaczynski, and Ted "Ted" Bundy. But the ensemble works best when we see the regulars yearn for a raise or promotion, struggle with Mary Tyler Moore's foibles and be there for Mary Tyler Moore when the going gets rough. I stole this from a review for *The Mary Tyler Moore Show*, but I think it completely and entirely makes sense to literally lift from that review and drop it into this context as well.

As someone with more quirky and alt tastes, I can't say that *America* is my favorite thing to watch. I'm more into *Breaking Bad*. Have you seen season 4?! Season 4 of *Breaking Bad* is flawless. Season 4 of *America* is VERY uneven. It had no main black characters. *Girls*, much?! I love *The Wire*!

I just hope to God (the American/right one) that they don't pull some deus-ex-machina shit at the end of this series. Like, there's nuclear war with North Korea, or they've been dead the whole time or something.

Anyway, it may have veered off wildly from the pilot, but *America* is definitely worth a look. It's an interesting experiment in the world of primetime sovereign nations. What the characters lack in consistency, they make up for in body weight, lingering racism, and inconsistency. But it makes for a quick and easy viewing, and can often surprise you with heartfelt turns. It's like eating Cool Ranch SpaghettiO's on a warm summer's eve. And hey, sometimes things get really good right before they're canceled.

MY RATING: 50 stars (out of 100).

———◦◦◦◦———

From: Myke Lewis
Date: Sun, Feb 19, 2012
Re: Death Star trash compactor

Hi, I'm only writing this because as of this minute, I have literally nothing better to do. I stumbled across your article by accident, and being a *Star Wars* fan (albeit one grounded in reality) I felt it warranted a read. I can't believe I'm doing this, but, I wanted to make two points:

1. I'm gonna go out on a limb here and guess that while Star Destroyers dump their garbage before light speed, it's possible that the Death Star has to recycle its material due primarily to its massive size (if I remember correctly, a Star Destroyer is 1.6 km long, with a crew of 50,000, and the Death Star is 128 km across with a crew of over a million people—I'm proud that I even kind of know that). It seems like resupplying the Death Star would be a massively inefficient undertaking (the Empire's attitude toward the environment aside, they are pretty efficient, as you said). Also, given the somewhat "secret" nature of the Death Star, they probably wouldn't want to impose a predictable resupply schedule on it, so as to prevent possible strikes against it. You could argue that the Battle of Yavin would shoot a hole in that theory, except that Grand Moff Tarkin willingly put the Death Star at the Rebellion's doorstep, so I still maintain that a routine resupply schedule would've been a detriment

to the safety of the Death Star (then again, so was having an easily accessible exhaust port, but that's a whole other thing).

2. Regarding the creature, while I'm not entirely sure why it's there either, I'm gonna guess at two things:

- If the Death Star does reclaim as much of its material as possible, then it would make sense to have an organism in there aiding with the reclamation and sanitation of the water in there (the same way they use bacterial slime to clean drinking water—gross, but it is a possibility maybe?).

- With regards to its being crushed by the walls (which, yeah, totally should've been one sided), there is that loud clanging sound, which, now that I think about it could've been the walls starting up, but I always thought it was a gate through which that creature entered the compactor opening and closing, thereby providing the necessary escape prior to crushingness.

And now that my virginity has apparently grown back, I shall go play *Bioshock* until my eyes bleed.

Keep writing. I enjoyed your article,
Myke

AFTER A THOROUGH BATTERY OF TESTS WE CAN NOW RECOMMEND "THE NEWSPAPER" AS THE BEST E-READER ON THE MARKET.

by JOHN FLOWERS

For the past three weeks our team of engineers has analyzed the most popular e-readers on the market in order to confer our annual "Editor's Choice" Award.

Devices were judged on a variety criteria to see how each functioned given a set of circumstances. The criteria themselves were weighted for the final score; individual and final grades were assigned on a curve.

Each device had its strengths. For some it was speed; for others it was capacity. Some were better with shorter articles; others with longer works. And cost, as always, was a factor. But in the end, one e-reader stood out.

The Newspaper.

The most obvious advantage of The Newspaper was the size of its display, which outclassed its rivals both in terms of size and elasticity. The Newspaper display could be read at full size or, when flipped open, twice its normal width. We also had no trouble reading copy when the display was flipped to half or even quarter size. One of our engineers even figured out how to make a hat.

One drawback to The Newspaper's display was that it used a much older version of the e-ink employed in some other e-reader displays. As a result, our hands became dirty and a bit oily after just a few minutes of use. However, further experimentation proved the device's sundry qualities, combined with the elasticity of its screen, to be a most effective weapon against flies. It also proved to be an adequate alternative to wrapping paper.

With the other e-readers, some of our engineers had the exact opposite experience. They reported an unwillingness to hold the device—nor let anyone else hold the device—unless their hands had been scrubbed and re-scrubbed and scrubbed again. The slightest grease mark or dust particle sent these engineers into a flying panic. Several are still checked in to a facility just outside the city.

What concerned us most about The Newspaper was its lack of wi-fi. Information on the system was locked, while on other e-readers it was open, ubiquitous, and current. Eventually, however, we found this advantage to be overstated, even misleading. Engineers using The Newspaper typically did so thirty to sixty minutes a day. Afterward, they went outside, formed relationships, and took in what life had to offer. Those using wi-fi-enabled e-readers tended to stay on the couch, scanning video sites for cats; eventually, downloading recipes for artichoke-cheese dip they'll never use.

There were other limits to The Newspaper's capabilities. Yet, these we could live with as well. Books could be downloaded onto the other e-readers, but after several days, we became bored with this feature. It seemed, for our tastes, that too many married professors with too many tenure problems were having too many midlife crises involving too many young mistresses. Also, we found that, even on a color monitor, we still couldn't finish *Swann's Way*.

Cost was a bit of a push. The Newspaper is more than some devices, when prorated over the course of two or more years, but inexpensive month-to-month. On the whole, users will have to determine which e-reader fits their budget best. However, we quickly discovered the e-reader's cheap short-term costs, coupled with its ubiquity and screen size, made for great cover when tailing people, like they did in the '30s.

The Newspaper also had other, unique features that added value to the overall experience.

The device's internal security system was chief among these attractions. We left one Newspaper on a park bench for six hours and, upon return, found it in the exact same place. Another we left in a bar after a thorough evening of testing. When we came back the next afternoon, The Newspaper remained untouched. The proprietor, incidentally, was curious why engineers would return for a day-old e-reader. We tried to explain the tests, but he gave us all dirty looks. When we tried to explain the process again, he became testy and said if we were going to bring that kind of claptrap in here, we could get the hell out. We did and went elsewhere to continue testing.

Battery life was also a plus, as The Newspaper lasted twenty-four hours—much longer than its next-best rival.

The Newspaper also has a great number of apps already downloaded onto the device, ones we have yet to see on any other e-reader. There are the previously mentioned fly-swatting, hat-making, present-wrapping, and tailing-people apps. But also the "same ol' bullshit," "who's got the sports section?," and "packing material for my eBay business" apps.

In the end, we found The Newspaper to be the least flashy and technical of the e-readers. Its value seems to be derived from a rather basic utility. And while we were generally pleased with the content, we would advise the makers of the next generation Newspaper to include a few new comic strips. That said, no other e-reader impressed us more—both in terms of convenience and fine hat-making.

SOCRATES AND GLAUCON ON THE HOME SHOPPING NETWORK.

by REBEKAH FRUMKIN

SOCRATES: Good evening, Glaucon. You look troubled.

GLAUCON: I am, Socrates.

SOCRATES: What worries you so?

GLAUCON: Look at my kitchen floor. That brown scum is the stain of fowl livers. I spilled them earlier today and cleaned them up, but the stains remain.

SOCRATES: I see.

GLAUCON: The stains are attracting countless pests with their foul odor and bacteria. There is no way to clean them up.

SOCRATES: Are you sure of that?

GLAUCON: Yes. To do so, I would need some convenient means of cleaning and sterilization.

SOCRATES: And you are convinced such a means does not exist?

GLAUCON: Socrates, I have lived in this city for the majority of my life, and, knowing the things I know, I do not think it is possible for something to clean and sterilize at the same time.

SOCRATES: Tell me, Glaucon, what does *clean* mean?

GLAUCON: Why, it means the opposite of dirty, Socrates.

SOCRATES: Surely it must mean something more than that.

GLAUCON: I don't understand, Socrates.

SOCRATES: If *clean* means the opposite of *dirty*, then to clean is to rid a space of dirt or plague, yes?

GLAUCON: Yes, Socrates.

SOCRATES: So cleanliness is the complete obliteration of dirt, bacteria, and unsightly stains. Am I right?

GLAUCON: Yes, Socrates.

SOCRATES: So to effectively clean, one must also sterilize, as a sterile surface is one that is also not dirty?

GLAUCON: Yes, Socrates.

SOCRATES: But an ordinary mop will not do this?

GLAUCON: No, Socrates. Look what a hassle it is for me to use! And none of the stains are coming off!

SOCRATES: Yes. It is quite impossible to get one's kitchen satisfactorily clean with an ordinary mop. But one could add Dirt-Fighting Technology™ to an ordinary mop, could he not?

GLAUCON: It depends on what sort of technology it is.

SOCRATES: It would consist of the elongation of the mop's bristles and an internal motor that causes the mop's head to swivel conveniently with the flip of a switch.

GLAUCON: Then yes, I agree that one could add such technology to an ordinary mop. But would it still be an ordinary mop, Socrates?

SOCRATES: Very astute, Glaucon. It would not. For convenience's sake, let's call it the EZ-Klean Mop™. Now answer me this: would the EZ-Klean Mop™, given that it has the Dirt-Fighting Technology™ I've just described, be able to more effectively rid spaces of dirt or plague?

GLAUCON: Yes.

SOCRATES: So you agree that it can clean better than an ordinary mop?

GLAUCON: I believe so.

SOCRATES: You're not fully convinced?

GLAUCON: I see that it can clean, but how will I sterilize my kitchen floor with it, Socrates? I need to get these stains out.

SOCRATES: I will answer your question with a question, Glaucon. What do you suppose the good men at Monsanto have been doing for the past fifteen years?

GLAUCON: I don't know, Socrates.

SOCRATES: They've been developing a Dirt-Fighting Formula™ that is stronger than any soap. This formula is safe to use in the home, and it can sterilize any surface. Do you suppose such a formula could increase the cleaning power of the EZ-Klean Mop™?

GLAUCON: Yes, Socrates.

SOCRATES: And you've already admitted that, with its longer bristles and swiveling head, the EZ-Klean Mop™ can clean far better than an ordinary mop, have you not?

GLAUCON: I have.

SOCRATES: And I've just said that the Dirt-Fighting Formula™, which is sold with the EZ-Klean Mop™, can sterilize any surface, have I not?

GLAUCON: You have.

SOCRATES: So it seems to me that such a thing exists which can both sterilize and clean: The EZ-Klean Mop™.

GLAUCON: Why, you're right, Socrates.

SOCRATES: Are you satisfied now, Glaucon?

GLAUCON: Well ... not just yet, Socrates. I'd like to own such a mop.

SOCRATES: You can, Glaucon. How much are you willing to pay for the EZ-Klean Mop™?

GLAUCON: Sixty dollars.

SOCRATES: But the mop only costs $49.99, Glaucon. As this is less than you were originally willing to pay, I assume you would willingly pay this amount.

GLAUCON: Yes, Socrates!

SOCRATES: Call the number at the bottom of your screen, Glaucon, and the EZ-Klean Mop™ will be shipped directly to your home. And if you call now, you'll receive a free can of SprayOn Hair™. Bald to fab in minutes!

GLAUCON: Thank you, Socrates! This will make my life so much easier!

SOCRATES: Do not thank me, Glaucon, for I have merely demonstrated to you what you already know about the EZ-Klean Mop™.

A PERSONAL ESSAY BY
A PERSONAL ESSAY.

by CHRISTY VANNOY

I am a Personal Essay and I was born with a port wine stain and beaten by my mother. A brief affair with a second cousin produced my first and only developmentally disabled child. Years of painful infertility would lead me straight into menopause and the hysterectomy I almost didn't survive.

I recently enrolled in a clinic led by the Article's Director and Editor for a national women's magazine. Technically, we were there to workshop and polish ourselves into submission. Secretly, though, we each hoped to out-devastate the other and nail ourselves a freelance contract.

I wasn't there to learn. I've been published as many times as I've been brutally sodomized, but I need to stay at the top of my game. Everyone thinks they have a story these days, and as soon as they let women in the Middle East start talking, you'll have to hold an editor hostage to get a response. Mark my words.

There were ten of us in the room. The Essay Without Arms worried me at first, but she had great bone structure and a wedding ring dangled from a chain on her neck, so I doubted her life has been all that hard.

Two male essays wandered in late. They were Homosexual Essays, a dime a dozen, and publishers aren't buying their battle with low self-esteem anymore. Even if their parents had kicked them out, I'd put money on a kind relative taking them in. It wasn't as if they'd landed in state care, like I had, and been delivered straight into the wandering hands of recently paroled foster parents. Being gay is about as tragic as a stray cuticle, and I wasn't born a Jehovah's Witness yesterday.

I presented my essay first, and tried not to look smug as I returned to my seat. The Article's Director let out a satisfied sigh and said, "I see someone's done this before." Yes, someone had. I've developed something of a reputation in the industry for taking meticulous notes on my suffering. It was a lesson learned the hard way after my year in sex slavery was rendered useless from the effects of crank on my long-term memory.

The third essay that read absolutely killed. She'd endured a series of miscarriages and narcoleptic seizures while living in a work camp during her youth in communist China. Initially, I was worried, but then I thought, whatever, good for her. There are twelve months in the year, and if Refugee Camp walked away with January, the April swimwear issue would be the perfect platform for my struggles with Exercise Bulimia. I don't mean to sound overly confident, but much of the unmitigated misfortune that has been my day-to-day life has taught me the importance of believing in myself.

Next up were two Divorce Essays, which came and went, forgettable at best. The Editor's critique suggested as much. Alopecia followed. She had promise, but was still clearly struggling for a hook. Every essay who's been through chemo or tried lesbianism ends up bald. Bald isn't the story. Alopecia was heading in the right direction, loving herself, but she was getting there all wrong. I think she needed to focus on not having eyelashes or pubic hair. Now that's interesting. That's an essay.

The last kid was unpublished and new on the circuit. It was hard to figure out what we were up against with this one. He walked up to the podium unassisted, bearing no visible signs of physical or mental retardation. Maybe it was something systemic, or worse still, the latest wave of competition to hit the market: a slow to diagnose mental illness. I tried to relax. It was hard to build story arcs off problems cured by pills. Problems caused by pills, on the other hand, sold on query alone. Shit. Maybe he was an addict.

His essay was weird. I think he was about a Tuesday. Not the Tuesday of an amputation, just a regular any old Tuesday. He persisted on beginning sentences without the personal pronoun *I* and comparing one thing to another instead of just out and out saying what happened. I was trying to track his word count but lost myself momentarily as he described the veins in a cashier's hands. It reminded me of my grandmother, her rough physical topography a testament to a life of hard work. We all leaned in during one of his especially long pauses, only to realize he wasn't pausing, he was done.

The Refugee Essay applauded loudly, but quite honestly, I think her tepid grip on English and admitted narcolepsy barred her from being a qualified judge. The Gay Essays joined in too, but they'll clap for anything with a penis and a Michelangelo jawline.

My ovations, on the other hand, are earned, and this essay never once told me how he felt about himself. Although, I have to admit, if I'd been him during that section where his father didn't even open the gift, I'd have been devastated by the rejection. Not of the thing itself, but of what it represented. Like it wasn't a gift so much as it was longing in the shape of a box, wrapped up in a bow.

Look, it wasn't like this essay didn't have potential. I think everyone in that room agreed he had a certain something. But talent takes time. Inoperable tumors just don't sprout up overnight, and psychotic breaks are nothing if not slow to boil.

The Article's Director didn't bother to give him any feedback. One of the Divorce Essays tried to pipe in about the unsatisfying ending, but the Editor silenced her with the stop sign of her raised palm. Wordlessly, she stared at this essay with a sorrow that reminded me of the last look the man I believed to be my father gave me before heading to Vietnam, only later to return a person wholly different from the one who left. "You deserve something better than this," the Editor said. "Yet for rules I follow, but did not create, I can't help you."

I thought about this essay a lot over the next few days, like he was beside me, equal parts familiar and strange. But the thing about life is that you simply cannot settle for melancholy, even when it's true. You are a not a Tragedy, you are a Personal Essay. You must rise above and you must do it in the last paragraph with basic grammar and easily recognized words.

Anyway, come November I will be buying every copy of *Marie Claire* I can get my one good hand on! You'll find me on page 124. If you haven't looked death straight in the eye or been sued by a sister wife, you won't see yourself in my story. But you will find solace in knowing your own problems are petty and banal. I have ascended victorious from the ashes of immeasurable self-doubt and pain. And I have not simply survived, I have flourished.

THE ULTIMATE GUIDE TO WRITING BETTER THAN YOU NORMALLY DO.

by COLIN NISSAN

WRITE EVERY DAY

Writing is a muscle. Smaller than a hamstring and slightly bigger than a bicep, and it needs to be exercised to get stronger. Think of your words as reps, your paragraphs as sets, your pages as daily workouts. Think of your laptop as a machine like the one at the gym where you open and close your inner thighs in front of everyone, exposing both your insecurities and your genitals. Because that is what writing is all about.

DON'T PROCRASTINATE

Procrastination is an alluring siren taunting you to google the country where Balki from *Perfect Strangers* was from, and to arrange sticky notes on your dog in the shape of hilarious dog shorts. A wicked temptress beckoning you to watch your children, and take showers. Well, it's time to look procrastination in the eye and tell that seafaring wench, "Sorry not today, today I write."

FIGHT THROUGH WRITER'S BLOCK

The blank white page. El Diablo Blanco. El Pollo Loco. Whatever you choose to call it, staring into the abyss in search of an idea can be terrifying. But ask yourself this: was Picasso intimidated by the blank canvas? Was Mozart intimidated by the blank sheet music? Was Edison intimidated by the blank light bulb? If you're still blocked up, ask yourself more questions, like: why did I quit my job at T.J. Maxx to write full-time? Can/should I eat this entire box of Apple Jacks? Is *The Price Is Right* on at ten or eleven?

LEARN FROM THE MASTERS

Mark Twain once said, "Show, don't tell." This is an incredibly important lesson for writers to remember; never get such a giant head that you feel entitled to throw around obscure phrases like, "Show, don't tell." Thanks for nothing, Mr. Cryptic.

FIND YOUR MUSE

Finding a really good muse these days isn't easy, so plan on going through quite a few before landing on a winner. Beware of muses who promise unrealistic timelines for your projects or who wear wizard clothes. When honing in on a promising new muse, also be on the lookout for other writers attempting to swoop in and muse-block you. Just be patient in your search, because the right muse/human relationship can last a lifetime.

HONE YOUR CRAFT

There are two things more difficult than writing. The first is editing, the second is expert-level Sudoku where there's literally two goddamned squares filled in. While editing is a grueling process, if you really work hard at it, in the end you may find that your piece has fewer words than it did before, which is great. Perhaps George Bernard Shaw said it best when upon sending a letter to a close friend, he wrote, "I'm sorry this letter is so long, I didn't have time to make it shorter." No quote better illustrates the point that writers are very busy.

ASK FOR FEEDBACK

It's so easy to hide in your little bubble, typing your little words with your little fingers on your little laptop from the comfort of your tiny chair in your miniature little house. I'm taking this tone to illustrate the importance of developing a thick skin. Remember, the only kind of criticism that doesn't make you a better writer is dishonest criticism. That, and someone telling you that you have weird shoulders.

READ, READ, READ

It's no secret that great writers are great readers, and that if you can't read, your writing will often suffer. Similarly, if you can read but have to move your lips to get through the longer words, you'll still be a pretty bad writer. Also, if you pronounce *espresso* like *expresso*.

STUDY THE RULES, THEN BREAK THEM

Part of finding your own voice as a writer is finding your own grammar. Don't spend your career lost in a sea of copycats when you can establish your own set of rules. If everyone's putting periods at the end of their sentences, put yours in the middle of words. Will it be incredibly difficult to read? Yes it will. Will it set you on the path to becoming a literary pioneer? Tough to say, but you're kind of out of options at this point.

KEEP IT TOGETHER

A writer's brain is full of little gifts, like a piñata at a birthday party. It's also full of demons, like a piñata at a birthday party in a mental hospital.

The truth is, it's demons that keep a tortured writer's spirit alive, not Tootsie Rolls. Sure, they'll give you a tiny burst of energy, but they won't do squat for your writing. So treat your demons with the respect they deserve, and with enough prescriptions to keep you wearing pants.

CONTRIBUTORS

MEGAN AMRAM is a television writer living in Los Angeles. She currently writes for *Parks and Recreation* and has previously written for *Kroll Show*, the MTV Movie Awards, and the Academy Awards. Her first book, *Science...for Her!*, is coming out later this year.

MATT BAER is an engineering student living in Tel Aviv. He saw *Star Wars* once as a kid, but wasn't really into it. However, he is really into arguing about *Star Wars*. He has always had trouble enjoying things for the right reasons.

Actor/filmmaker/author/stand-up comedian MICHAEL IAN BLACK is starring on the upcoming Fox series *Us and Them* and cohosting TBS's new *Trust Me, I'm a Game Show Host*. He's best known for his Comedy Central stand-up specials and the numerous films, books, and TV series he's written, starred in, directed, and/or created.

KATIE BRINKWORTH is a writer living in San Francisco. She works in advertising and draws inspiration from its absurdity.

ANDY BRYAN is a recovering anthropologist who may be found aimlessly wandering the desert wastelands of Arizona. His work has appeared in various online and print publications of questionable repute. He packs a bullwhip, but abstains from crystal skulls.

LUKE BURNS is a writing guy who does writing things in New York City. You can read some more of his writing things at *lukevburns.com*. His work was also included in *The McSweeney's Book of Politics and Musicals*.

JESSE EISENBERG is an Academy Award–nominated actor, playwright, and humorist for the *New Yorker*. He has written the plays *Asuncion* and *The Revisionist*, which starred Vanessa Redgrave, and has appeared in the films *Now You See Me*, *The Social Network*, *Adventureland*, *Zombieland*, and *The Squid and the Whale*.

Born without any superpowers, SETH FISHER has carved out a "career" as a sports blogger (*MGoBlog*) and publisher/editor of indie preview magazines. The remainder goes into a growing family, volunteer organizing around Detroit, and keeping the internet safe from wrong people.

JOHN FLOWERS has written for *McSweeney's* and the *New Yorker*. John worked at *Time* magazine for seven years before falling ass-backward into a producer's gig in TV news. He lives in Brooklyn but drinks globally. Follow him @MrJohnFlowers.

JOSH FREEDMAN is a writer and economic policy researcher living in Washington, D.C. He knows far too much about pension reform and, as a result, is a terrible person to bring to a party.

REBEKAH FRUMKIN is a student at the Iowa Writers' Workshop, and her one MVP moment of recent years was having a short story featured in *The Best American Nonrequired Reading* 2009. Now she teaches fiction writing at the University of Iowa and lives in Iowa City with her boyfriend, a ginger geologist whose ambivalence about being featured in this bio she has ignored. She's currently at work on a novel about drugs, mental illness, and conspiracy theories in Ohio.

MEREDITH K. GRAY's work has appeared in *Image*, *The Normal School*, and *NANO Fiction*. She received her MFA from Vanderbilt University, and has held residencies at Kimmel Harding Nelson Center for the Arts and Interlochen, where she taught humor writing. She lives in Baltimore.

ERIC HAGUE is a writer who lives near Philadelphia.

KATE HAHN is a journalist and humor writer in Los Angeles. Some of her favorite reporting gigs require international travel and wellies. Her yellow fever vaccine is up-to-date. She studied the funny at The Second City and Groundlings.

TIM HUNDSDORFER lives in Lyon, France, with his wife, Susan, and greyhound, Ned. After contracting Hashimoto's Encephalopathy, a rare brain disease, he was left by his first wife, fired from his job, and thrown out of the PhD program at the University of Colorado. Really, man, that's how it went down.

MATTHEW DUVERNE HUTCHINSON is a writer and television producer in Atlanta, Georgia. But enough about him, let's talk about you.

JORY JOHN is the author of the forthcoming picture books *I Will Chomp You* (Random House) and *Goodnight, Already!* (HarperCollins) and co-author of *All My Friends Are Dead*, *I Feel Relatively Neutral About New York*, *All My Friends Are Still Dead*, *K is for Knifeball*, and *Pirate's Log* (Chronicle Books). Jory edited *Thanks and Have Fun Running the Country: Kids' Letters to President Obama* (McSweeney's) and has written for the *New York Times*, the *San Francisco Chronicle*, the *Believer*, and other publications.

BEN JURNEY was born in New York City in 1991. His writing has been featured on *Wired* and *FilmDrunk* and at the Upright Citizens Brigade Theatre in New York. He is currently a senior at Skidmore College.

ELLIE KEMPER is a writer and performer who divides her time among New York, Los Angeles, and the white sand beaches of Bora Bora.

DAN KENNEDY is a writer living in New York. He is author of the novel *American Spirit*, the memoirs *Loser Goes First* and *Rock On* (a *Times of London* Book of the Year). He is host of *The Moth* storytelling podcast, both a performer and host at live Moth events, and his stories have been featured on the Peabody Award–winning *Moth Radio Hour*. His work has appeared in *GQ* and numerous anthologies. More at *dankennedynyc.com*.

RACHEL KLEIN was born and raised in Chicago, Illinois. Her childhood crushes were Johnny Dangerously and Jo from *The Facts of Life*. She currently lives in Boston, Massachusetts, where she writes and performs comedy and teaches high school English.

MIKE LACHER is a writer and developer in New York City. You can find more of his work at *mikelacher.com*.

ALYSSA LANG is an associate professor of graphic design living in Monrovia, California, with her husband, John, and son, Beckett. She designs posters and other printed ephemera, combining type and images both digitally and via letterpress. Learn more at *littleutopia.com*.

MYKE LEWIS is a full-time musician, music journalist, and essayist, as well as an occasional university lecturer. When he isn't doing any of those things, he can be found yelling at children or shaking his fist at the gods. Read more here: *kill-a-dj.com*.

KRISTINA LOEW is a satirist and social commentator who has written extensively about politics, the economy, and American culture. Her early work, obituaries detailing the wonderful and productive lives of people who hadn't died yet, has recently been published.

CHRISTOPHER MAH lives, works, and writes in Seattle. His writing has been published in *The Bygone Bureau*, *Yankee Pot Roast*, and *Splitsider*, and has been adapted for NPR's *Marketplace*. It irritates him when writers refer to themselves in the third person

PASHA MALLA is the author of four books. He lives in Canada.

OYL MILLER is an advertising copywriter from Portland, Oregon, currently working for Wieden+Kennedy in Tokyo, Japan. Miller has created campaigns for Nike, PlayStation, Google, and other clients.

JOHN MOE is the host of the public radio show *Wits* and author of the "Pop Song Correspondences" column on McSweeney's Internet Tendency. He lives in Minnesota on purpose.

WENDY MOLYNEUX lives in Los Angeles and writes for the TV show *Bob's Burgers* and the radio program *Wits*. She also contributes semi-frequently to McSweeney's Internet Tendency and the *Rumpus*'s Funny Women column.

ROSS MURRAY lives on the Canada-US border in Stanstead, Quebec, where he writes weekly for the *Sherbrooke Record* and contributes regularly to CBC Radio and *lifeinquebec.com*. Ross's latest collection, *Don't Everyone Jump At Once*, is published by Blue Ice Books.

COLIN NISSAN is a humor writer and regular contributor to McSweeney's Internet Tendency. He has also written for the *New Yorker* and is a headline contributor for the *Onion*. You can follow his writing @cnissan.

JOHN ORTVED, an outspoken atheist and moron, lives between Canada, New York City, and Twitter @jortved. He contributes to the *New Yorker*, *Vanity Fair*, and the *New York Times*, among other publications, and blogs about bears (they're fun!).

JOHN K. PECK is a writer, musician, and printer. Along with his wife, he is co-owner of Volta Press and co-editor of *Beeswax Magazine*. He can be found online at *johnkpeck.com*.

JASON ROEDER is a writer for *adultswim.com* and a former senior writer for the *Onion*. He is also the author of the satirical self-help manual *Oh, the Humanity!: A Gentle Guide to Social Interaction for the Feeble Young Introvert*.

KARI ANNE ROY lives a life of mayhem in Austin, Texas, with her husband and three charmingly malevolent children. She enjoys reading (and writing!) lots of books, contributing wildly inappropriate essays to McSweeney's Internet Tendency, and eating lots of tacos.

A member of the editorial staff at *Vanity Fair* magazine, MIKE SACKS is the author of *Your Wildest Dreams, Within Reason*, and *And Here's the Kicker: Conversations with 21 Humor Writers on their Craft*. The co-author of *SEX: Our Bodies, Our Junk* and the co-editor of *Care to Make Love in That Gross Little Space Between Cars?*, his work has appeared in *McSweeney's*, the *New York Times*, the *Washington Post*, the *New Yorker*, *Time*, *Esquire*, *Vanity Fair*, *GQ*, *Radar*, the *Believer*, *Vice*, and *Salon*, among others.

ANTHONY SAMS, a graduate of Indiana University and the University of North Carolina Wilmington, has published fiction and poetry less frequently since becoming an assistant professor of English at Ivy Tech Community College.

SARAH SCHMELLING has written for the *New York Times*, the *Washington Post*, *Salon*, *Slate*, *Parents* magazine, and many other publications, and she is the author of a humor book. She lives with her family outside of Washington, D.C.

TIM STREISEL is forty-six, married with two sons, and lives on the outskirts of St. Louis. He is an electrical engineer and a lifelong *Star Wars* geek who is fond of ice hockey, diesel trucks, and the finer-quality whiskeys.

MELINDA TAUB is a writer in New York City. Her work has appeared in the *Onion*, *Billy on the Street*, and at the Upright Citizens Brigade. Her first novel, *Still Star-Crossed*, was published this summer. Follow her on Twitter @melindataub.

J. M. TYREE has contributed to *Lapham's Quarterly*, the *Believer*, *Sight & Sound*, and the Film Classics series of books from the British Film Institute. He is an editor for *New England Review*.

CHRISTY VANNOY lives in New York City. Her writing has appeared on McSweeney's Internet Tendency and in *The Best American Essays of 2011*.

SARAH WALKER is a comedy writer and author living in Los Angeles. McSweeney's Internet Tendency launched her writing career by taking a chance on an unknown kid, and for that she thinks they are the bee's knees. She loves cake.

SEAN WALSH is a theater educator from Somerville, Mass. He holds an MFA from Lesley University in YA Fiction. His play, *A Game of Chicken*, was selected as a KCACTF semifinalist and was produced for the 2012 Boston Theater Marathon.

TEDDY WAYNE is the author of the novels *The Love Song of Jonny Valentine* and *Kapitoil*. A Whiting Writers' Award recipient, his work regularly appears in the *New Yorker*, the *New York Times*, and his McSweeney's column, "Teddy Wayne's Unpopular Proverbs."

JOHN FRANK WEAVER lives in Portsmouth, New Hampshire, with his wife and two kids. His first book, *Robots Are People Too*, was published in 2013 by Praeger Publishing. Follow him @RobotsRPeople.

ACKNOWLEDGMENTS

A special thanks to past editors of McSweeney's Internet Tendency, who include: Kevin Shay, Lee Epstein, Gideon Lewis-Kraus, Ed Page, and B.R. Cohen.